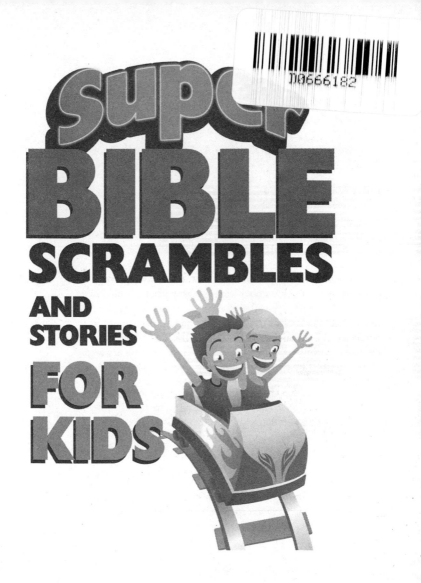

super BIBLE SCRAMBLES

AND STORIES

FOR KIDS

Bible Scrambles © 2001 by Barbour Publishing, Inc.
Super Silly Stories © 2000 by Barbour Publishing, Inc.

Super Bible Scrambles and Stories for Kids © 2009 by Barbour
Publishing, Inc.

ISBN 978-1-60260-396-7

Published by Barbour Publishing, Inc., P.O. Box 719, Uhrichsville,
Ohio 44683, www.barbourbooks.com

*Our mission is to publish and distribute inspirational products offering
exceptional value and biblical encouragement to the masses.*

Member of the
Evangelical Christian
Publishers Association

Printed in the United States of America.

Super BIBLE SCRAMBLES AND STORIES FOR KIDS

BARBOUR
PUBLISHING

A DIFFERENT KIND OF FRUIT

"BUT THE FRUIT OF THE SPIRIT IS LOVE, JOY, PEACE, PATIENCE, KINDNESS, GOODNESS, FAITHFULNESS, GENTLENESS AND SELF-CONTROL. AGAINST SUCH THINGS THERE IS NO LAW."

GALATIANS 5:22

WHAT DOES GOD MEAN WHEN HE TALKS ABOUT THE *FRUIT OF THE SPIRIT?*

IN JOHN 15:1–8, JESUS CALLS HIMSELF THE VINE AND HIS DISCIPLES THE BRANCHES. HE TELLS US THAT IF WE REMAIN IN HIM, HE WILL REMAIN IN US AND WE WILL BEAR MUCH FRUIT; APART FROM JESUS (THE VINE), WE (THE BRANCHES) CANNOT BEAR FRUIT BY OURSELVES. WE MUST *REMAIN IN THE VINE.*

ELSEWHERE IN GOD'S WORD, WE HEAR JESUS SAYING THAT IF WE REMAIN IN HIM WE WILL BEAR MUCH FRUIT. HOW DOES ONE REMAIN IN JESUS? HOW DOES ONE BEAR THE FRUIT OF THE SPIRIT?

AS YOU GO THROUGH THE ACTIVITIES IN THIS BOOK, LET GOD SHOW YOU WHAT IT MEANS TO REMAIN IN JESUS AND HOW YOU MAY BEAR THE FRUIT OF THE SPIRIT IN YOUR LIFE.

LOVE

WHAT IS LOVE? IS LOVE JUST A *FEELING* OR IS IT AN ACTION? IS LOVE BOTH A FEELING AND AN ACTION?

WE KNOW WE LOVE OUR PARENTS, OUR BROTHERS, OUR SISTERS, OR OUR FRIENDS. WHAT ABOUT WHEN THEY MAKE US ANGRY OR HURT OUR FEELINGS? DO WE STILL *FEEL* LOVE FOR THEM AT THAT MOMENT?

HOW DO YOU FEEL WHEN THE KIDS AT SCHOOL ARE MEAN TO YOU AND YOUR BEST FRIEND JOINS IN WITH THEM? DO YOU STILL *FEEL* LOVE FOR THEM OR DO YOU FEEL ANGRY, AFRAID, AND HURT?

WHAT OF JESUS WHEN HE WAS DYING ON THE CROSS? DO YOU THINK HE FELT LOVE FOR THOSE WHO WERE MAKING FUN OF HIM AND INSULTING HIM?

REMEMBER WHAT JESUS SAID BEFORE HE DIED: "FATHER, FORGIVE THEM, FOR THEY DO NOT KNOW NOT WHAT THEY ARE DOING."

IT WAS BY THESE WORDS *AND ACTIONS* THAT JESUS SHOWED HIS LOVE, EVEN FOR THOSE WHO CRUCIFIED HIM. HOW DO YOU THINK HE WAS ABLE TO DO THIS AFTER EVERYTHING HE WENT THROUGH?

DO YOU THINK HE DID THIS BY HIS OWN STRENGTH AND WILL, OR WAS HIS FATHER DOING IT *THROUGH* HIM?

IN THE NEW TESTAMENT, JESUS' COMMANDS TO US BOTH HAD TO DO WITH LOVE. DO YOU KNOW WHAT THOSE COMMANDS ARE?

SCRAMBLED VERSES

UNSCRAMBLE THE WORDS BELOW AND COMPLETE THE VERSE ON THE NEXT PAGE.

"EOVL SI TENITPA, LEVO SI INKD. TI SOED TNO VENY, TI OSED TNO SOABT, TI SI TON RDOUP. TI SI OTN ERDU, TI SI ONT FESL-KESENGI, TI SI ONT LSAIEY RGNEDEA, TI EPSEK ON RRCEDO FO SORNGW. VLOE DSEO NOT GLHTDIE NI LVIE TBU CRESEJIO WHIT HET UTRHT. TI WYAASL COTRESTP, LYAWSA UTSSRT, AAWSYL EOPSH, SALAYW SVRSEREPEE."

1 CORINTHIANS 13:4-7

SCRAMBLED CIRCLES

UNSCRAMBLE THE WORDS FROM THE LIST BELOW. THEN USE THE CIRCLED LETTERS ON THE NEXT PAGE TO COMPLETE THE VERSE.

1. RIITPS

2. ETGIHDL

3. NRITEE

4. YUINT

5. FEERCTP

6. RCREDO

7. KSEE

10

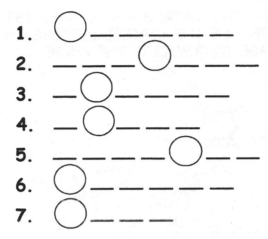

1. ◯ _ _ _ _ _
2. _ _ _ ◯ _ _ _
3. _ ◯ _ _ _ _
4. _ ◯ _ _ _
5. _ _ _ _ ◯ _ _
6. ◯ _ _ _ _
7. ◯ _ _ _

"BUT GOD DEMONSTRATES HIS OWN LOVE FOR US IN THIS: WHILE WE WERE STILL __ __ __ __ __ __ __, CHRIST DIED FOR US."

ROMANS 5:8

11

SCRAMBLED CIRCLES

UNSCRAMBLE THE WORDS FROM THE LIST BELOW. THEN USE THE CIRCLED LETTERS ON THE NEXT PAGE TO COMPLETE THE VERSE.

1. THRUT

2. AOFRVEG

3. ETHAFR

4. DMIYTITI

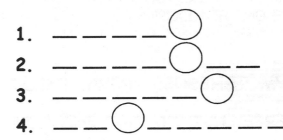

1. _ _ _ _ ◯

2. _ _ _ _ ◯ _ _

3. _ _ _ _ _ ◯

4. _ _ ◯ _ _ _ _ _

"LOVE DOES NO __ __ __ __ TO ITS NEIGHBOR. THEREFORE LOVE IS THE FULFILLMENT OF THE LAW."

ROMANS 13:10

SCRAMBLED VERSES

UNSCRAMBLE THE WORDS BELOW AND COMPLETE
THE VERSE ON THE NEXT PAGE.

"UYO, YM TRHESOBR, REWE EALDCL

OT EB ERFE. UBT OD TNO EUS ROYU

DOERMFE OT GLDUENI ETH FNLUSI

RTNAEU; HEARRT, RSEEV NEO

NTOARHE NI VOEL. HET EETIRN WLA

SI SEMUMD PU NI A ILESGN

NCOMDMA: 'EOVL RYOU BHIGEORN SA

ORSULEYF.'"

"_____, ____ ____ _____,

_____ _____ ____ ____ ____

_____. ____ ____ ____ ____

_____ ____ _____

_____ _____ _____

_____ _____;

_____, _____ ____ ____

_____ ____ _____.

____ ____ _____ ____ ____

_____ ____ ____ ____ ____

_____ _____;

.
_____ _____ _____

____ _____.'"

GALATIANS 5:13-14

15

SCRAMBLED VERSES

UNSCRAMBLE THE WORDS BELOW AND COMPLETE
THE VERSE ON THE NEXT PAGE.

"REAB TIWH CEAH HETRO DAN
GRVEIFO VTEERWAH IVEACENSRG
OYU AYM HAEV NIGAATS NEO
OEHTRAN. OEVIRFG AS HET ROLD
EAORGVF UYO. NAD VROE LAL TEESH
SVTUERI TPU NO OLEV, HHIWC NBISD
MHET LLA OGERTTEH NI TRPECEF
NYTIU."

COLOSSIANS 3:13–14

17

SCRAMBLED CIRCLES

UNSCRAMBLE THE WORDS FROM THE LIST BELOW. THEN USE THE CIRCLED LETTERS ON THE NEXT PAGE TO COMPLETE THE VERSE.

1. FUINLS

2. DRIEP

3. UIRVET

4. NREGA

5. NSI

6. ERET

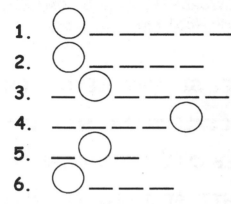

1. ◯ __ __ __ __ __
2. ◯ __ __ __ __
3. __ ◯ __ __ __ __
4. __ __ __ __ ◯
5. __ ◯ __
6. ◯ __ __ __

"FOR GOD DID NOT GIVE US A SPIRIT OF TIMIDITY, BUT A __ __ __ __ __ __ OF POWER, OF LOVE AND OF SELF-DISCIPLINE."

2 TIMOTHY 1:7

SCRAMBLED VERSES

UNSCRAMBLE THE WORDS BELOW AND COMPLETE THE VERSE ON THE NEXT PAGE.

"WHO TRAGE SI HET LEVO TEH AHRETF SHA DSALEVIH NO SU, HTTA EW DUSLOH EB CLDAEL IECNRDHL FO DGO! NAD AHTT SI THAW EW AER! HET SRONAE ETH LWRDO EDSO TNO OKNW SU SI THTA TI DDI NTO NKWO MHI."

"_____ _____ _____ ____ _____

_____ _____ ____ _____

_____ _____ _____ _

____ , _____ ____ _____

_____ _____ _____

_____ _____ ! ____ _____

_____ _____ _____ _ _____ !

_____ ___ _____

_____ ___ _____

_____ ___ ___ ____

____ ___ ____ ____ _____

____ . "

1 JOHN 3:1

21

SCRAMBLED VERSES

UNSCRAMBLE THE WORDS BELOW AND COMPLETE
THE VERSE ON THE NEXT PAGE.

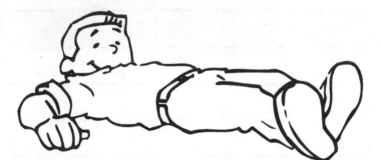

"STHI SI WHO EW KWNO THWA VLEO

SI: SESUJ RTSIHC DLIA ONWD SIH

EILF RFO SU. DAN EW GTUHO OT

YLA WDON URO ELVIS OFR UOR

EOBTRHSR."

"_____ _____ _____

_____ _____ ___: _____

_____ _____ _____

_____ _____ _____ _____.

_____ _____ _____ _____

_____ _____ _____ _____ _____

_____ _____ _____."

1 JOHN 3:16

SCRAMBLED CIRCLES

UNSCRAMBLE THE WORDS FROM THE LIST BELOW. THEN USE THE CIRCLED LETTERS ON THE NEXT PAGE TO COMPLETE THE VERSE.

1. OWH
2. EJERCIO
3. EDAR
4. GHELDIT
5. LOSU

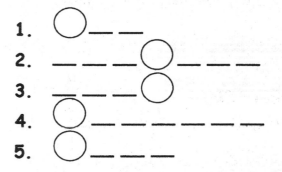

1. ◯ __ __
2. __ __ __ ◯ __ __ __
3. __ __ __ ◯
4. ◯ __ __ __ __ __
5. ◯ __ __ __

"DEAR CHILDREN, LET US NOT LOVE WITH __ __ __ __ __ OR TONGUE BUT WITH ACTIONS AND IN TRUTH."

1 JOHN 3:18

SCRAMBLED VERSES

UNSCRAMBLE THE WORDS BELOW AND COMPLETE THE VERSE ON THE NEXT PAGE.

"ARED DESNRFI, TEL SU OELV EON THRANOE, RFO EOVL OESMC MROF DGO. EYEONREV HOW SVLOE SHA ENBE BNRO FO OGD NAD NSKWO GDO. VEEHOWR OSDE TNO LEOV OSED TON ONKW DGO, ASCEBUE ODG SI EVLO."

26

"_____ _____, _____

___ _____ ____ _____,

___ _____ ___ _____ ___.

_____ ___ ___ _____

_____ _____ ___

_____ ___ _____ ___.

_____ ___ ___

_____ ___ ____ ___

___, _____ ___ __

_____."

1 JOHN 4:7–8

27

SCRAMBLED VERSES

UNSCRAMBLE THE WORDS BELOW AND COMPLETE
THE VERSE ON THE NEXT PAGE.

"RTEHE SI ON AFRE NI EOVL. UTB
CPTREEF VLEO VDSREI UTO EFRA,
EBUESAC ERAF ASH OT OD TWIH
THNPUEMISN. ETH NOE HWO RFSEA
SI ONT DMEA CETPERF NI VOLE."

"_____ _____ _____ _____

_____ _____. _____ _____

_____ _____ _____

_____, _____ _____

_____ _____ _____ _____

_____. _____

_____ _____ _____ _____

_____ _____ _____

_____ _____."

1 JOHN 4:18

29

THINK, THINK, THINK

GOD LOVES US AND WILL NEVER STOP LOVING US. GOD'S LOVE FOR US IS NOT BASED ON WHAT WE DO OR DON'T DO. GOD KNOWS OUR THOUGHTS AND, EVEN WITH OUR WRONG THOUGHTS, *LOVES US ANYWAY.*

GOD INVITES YOU TO BELONG TO HIM. YOUR NAME IS ON HIS INVITATION LIST. TO BE INVITED IS TO BE VALUED, AND IF YOU DON'T COME, YOU WILL BE MISSED. TO BE INVITED IS TO BE WANTED, AND IF YOU DO COME, YOU WILL BE WELCOMED. TO BE INVITED IS TO BE FREE, AND GOD WILL RESPECT YOUR CHOICE.

YOU ARE NOT AN OUTSIDER WITH GOD. YOU ARE IMPORTANT TO HIM AND LOVED JUST THE WAY YOU ARE.

GOD HAS *ALWAYS* LOVED YOU, AND HE NOW INVITES YOU TO COME AND RECEIVE HIS LOVE.

GOD LOVES YOU SO MUCH THAT HE SENT YOU HIS ONE AND ONLY SON, THAT IF YOU BELIEVE IN THE ONE HE SENT, HE WILL GIVE YOU ETERNAL LIFE, AND YOU WILL BE CALLED A CHILD OF GOD.

THERE IS ONLY ONE THAT CAN LOVE YOU PERFECTLY AND THAT IS GOD. HIS PERFECT LOVE CHASES ALL FEAR AWAY, AND HE WANTS YOU TO EXPERIENCE HIS LOVE AND LET HIS LOVE LIVE *THROUGH* YOU TO OTHERS BY THE HOLY SPIRIT.

GOD WANTS TO PUT HIS LOVE IN YOUR HEART. WOULD *YOU* BE WILLING TO ACCEPT GOD'S INVITATION?

WHAT IS JOY? IS JOY SOMETHING THAT ONE FEELS, OR DOES IT COME IN KNOWING TRUTH?

DO YOU THINK JESUS WAS FEELING JOY WHILE HE HUNG ON THE CROSS DYING? GOD'S WORD TELLS US THAT FOR THE *JOY SET BEFORE HIM*, JESUS FACED SUFFERING ON THE CROSS.

HOW COULD THERE BE ANY JOY IN DYING ON A CROSS? HIS JOY CAME FROM KNOWING THAT BY HIS DEATH HE WAS GIVING YOU AND ME A WAY TO BE AT PEACE WITH GOD. WE ALL HAVE FALLEN SHORT OF THE GLORY OF GOD. EVERY ONE OF US HAS SINNED AND DONE THINGS WRONG.

JESUS PAID THE PRICE FOR ALL OF OUR SINS. HE DID NOTHING WRONG, YET HE DIED ON THE CROSS FOR ALL OF US. IT SHOULD HAVE BEEN US NAILED TO THAT CROSS, BECAUSE THE PENALTY FOR OUR SIN IS *DEATH*!

JESUS LOVED US SO MUCH THAT HE WAS WILLING TO TAKE OUR PLACE ON THE CROSS, AND SO, HE DIED FOR OUR SINS.

NOW THERE IS *NOTHING MORE* THAT NEEDS TO BE DONE. AS JESUS SPOKE FROM THE CROSS, HIS WORDS WERE, "IT IS FINISHED." THE PRICE FOR SIN WAS PAID IN FULL.

HOW DOES THAT MAKE YOU FEEL KNOWING THIS? DOES IT MAKE YOU HAPPY, DELIGHTED, OR EXCITED? DOES IT GIVE YOU COMFORT AND MAKE YOU WANT TO REJOICE?

THIS IS JOY.

SCRAMBLED CIRCLES

UNSCRAMBLE THE WORDS FROM THE LIST BELOW. THEN USE THE CIRCLED LETTERS ON THE NEXT PAGE TO COMPLETE THE VERSE.

1. RDLOW
2. OEUTGN
3. SEUJS
4. GUHOT
5. ISH
6. LEMOCPTE
7. EHPO

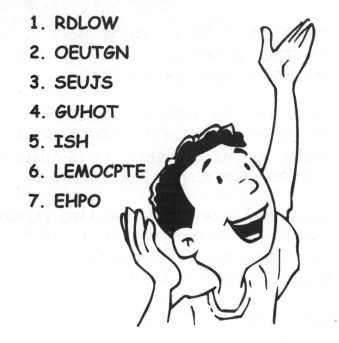

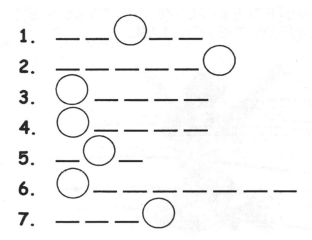

1. __ __ ◯ __ __

2. __ __ __ __ ◯

3. ◯ __ __ __ __

4. ◯ __ __ __ __

5. __ ◯ __

6. ◯ __ __ __ __ __

7. __ __ __ ◯

"THEN MY SOUL WILL __ __ __ __ __ __
IN THE LORD AND DELIGHT IN HIS
SALVATION."

PSALM 35:9

SCRAMBLED VERSES

UNSCRAMBLE THE WORDS BELOW AND COMPLETE THE VERSE ON THE NEXT PAGE.

"ETNH IWLL I GO OT HTE AARTL

FO DGO, OT DGO, YM OYJ NDA YM

TDGEHLI. I LWLI ESRPIA UYO HWTI

EHT PHRA, O OGD, YM DGO."

"_____ _____ _____ _____ _____

_____ _____ _____ _____

_____, _____ _____, _____

_____ _____ _____ _____.

_____ _____ _____ _____ _____

_____ _____ _____ _____, _____

_____, _____ _____."

PSALM 43:4

37

UNSCRAMBLE THE WORDS FROM THE LIST BELOW. THEN USE THE CIRCLED LETTERS ON THE NEXT PAGE TO COMPLETE THE VERSE.

1. HSRTIC
2. ELVO
3. RMFO
4. PRWEO
5. ADLE
6. AFRE
7. TCNIOA
8. HRATE

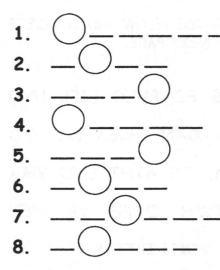

1. ◯ __ __ __ __ __
2. __ ◯ __ __
3. __ __ __ ◯
4. ◯ __ __ __ __
5. __ __ ◯
6. __ ◯ __ __
7. __ __ ◯ __ __ __
8. __ ◯ __ __ __

"I HAVE TOLD YOU THIS SO THAT MY
JOY MAY BE IN YOU AND THAT YOUR
JOY MAY BE __ __ __ __ __ __ __ __."

JOHN 15:11

SCRAMBLED VERSES

UNSCRAMBLE THE WORDS BELOW AND COMPLETE THE VERSE ON THE NEXT PAGE.

"YMA EHT ODG FO PHEO LIFL UYO HITW LAL OJY DAN EPCEA SA UYO STRTU NI IHM, OS ATHT UYO YMA OOLVREFW ITWH OHPE YB HET EPROW FO HTE YOLH IPTIRS."

40

"_____ _____ _____ _____

_____ _____ _____

_____ _____ _____ _____

_____ _____ _____ _____

_____ _____, _____ _____

_____ _____ _____

_____ _____ _____ _____ _____

_____ _____ _____ _____ _____

_____."

ROMANS 15:13

SCRAMBLED VERSES

UNSCRAMBLE THE WORDS BELOW AND COMPLETE
THE VERSE ON THE NEXT PAGE.

"FI OUY VHAE NYA TENECNMOEUGRA

RMOF GBNIE DUENIT TWHI HTSRIC,

FI YAN ROOTFMC OFMR IHS OELV, IF

NAY IFLEPLWHSO THIW ETH ISIRPT,

FI   NYA   ENENERDSTS   DAN

SMCOSAIPNO, NTEH KMEA YM OJY

EPMOLCTE YB NEIBG EIKL-DDNIME,

VHNGIA ETH MSAE VLEO, NGBIE NEO

NI TRPSII DAN PPSRUOE."

"_____ _____ _____ _____ _____
_____ _____ _____
_____ _____ _____ _____
_____, _____ _____ _____
_____ _____ _____, _____
_____ _____ _____ _____
_____ _____, _____ _____
_____ _____ _____
_____, _____ _____ _____
_____ _____ _____ _____ _____
_____ _____ - _____,
_____ _____ _____ _____ _____,
_____ _____ _____ _____
_____ _____ _____. "

PHILIPPIANS 2:1-2

43

SCRAMBLED VERSES

UNSCRAMBLE THE WORDS BELOW AND COMPLETE
THE VERSE ON THE NEXT PAGE.

"UYO CMBEEA RMTSTIAIO FO SU DNA

FO HTE DLRO; NI TPSEI FO RSEVEE

GFRNFSUEI, UYO MDLWCEEO HTE

GEESASM HWTI HET YOJ NGVEI BY

HET YHLO TSRPII."

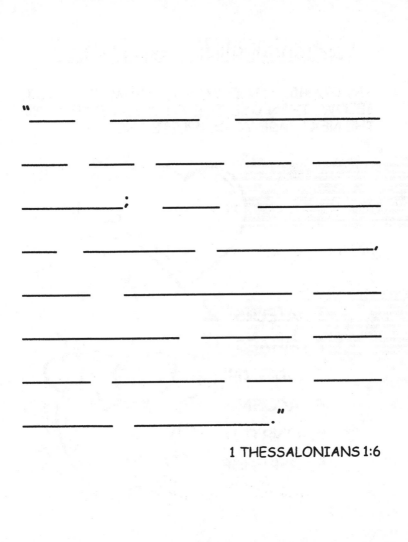

1 THESSALONIANS 1:6

45

SCRAMBLED CIRCLES

UNSCRAMBLE THE WORDS FROM THE LIST BELOW. THEN USE THE CIRCLED LETTERS ON THE NEXT PAGE TO COMPLETE THE VERSE.

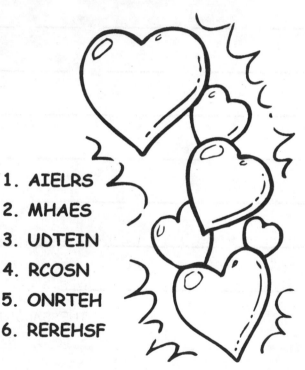

1. AIELRS

2. MHAES

3. UDTEIN

4. RCOSN

5. ONRTEH

6. REREHSF

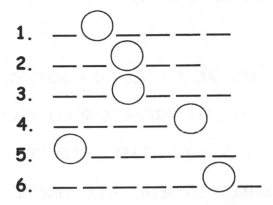

1. _ ◯ _ _ _ _
2. _ _ ◯ _ _
3. _ _ ◯ _ _ _
4. _ _ _ _ ◯
5. ◯ _ _ _ _ _
6. _ _ _ _ _ ◯ _

"YOUR LOVE HAS GIVEN ME GREAT JOY
AND ENCOURAGEMENT, BECAUSE YOU,
BROTHER, HAVE REFRESHED THE HEARTS
OF THE __ __ __ __ __ __."

PHILEMON 1:7

SCRAMBLED VERSES

UNSCRAMBLE THE WORDS BELOW AND COMPLETE
THE VERSE ON THE NEXT PAGE.

"TLE SU XFI ROU YSEE NO SJEUS,

ETH RAOUTH DNA RREEETCFP FO RUO

TFHIA, HWO RFO EHT YJO TSE

EEFROB IHM DDRNEUE HTE SROSC,

GSNNICRO SIT MEHSA, DAN TSA

NWDO TA HTE HRGTI NHDA FO HET

NHEOTR FO DGO."

HEBREWS 12:2

49

THINK, THINK, THINK

WHEN YOU ACCEPT GOD'S INVITATION, YOUR HEART WILL BE FILLED WITH JOY—A JOY THAT ONLY GOD CAN GIVE YOU.

YOU ARE A CHILD OF GOD. YOU ARE BEAUTIFUL; YOU ARE A DELIGHT AND A JOY TO HIM. GOD REJOICES IN THE FACT THAT YOU ARE NOW HIS CHILD. YOU BRING GOD MUCH HAPPINESS AND DELIGHT. GOD KNOWS HIS CHILD HAS NOW COME HOME.

EVERY TIME SOMEONE ANSWERS GOD'S INVITATION TO BECOME HIS CHILD, ALL OF HEAVEN REJOICES WITH GOD. NOTHING MAKES GOD HAPPIER AND FILLS HIM WITH GREATER JOY THAN KNOWING YOU ARE HIS CHILD.

ONCE YOU ARE GOD'S CHILD, THERE IS NOTHING THAT CAN TAKE YOU AWAY FROM HIM OR NOTHING YOU CAN DO THAT WILL MAKE HIM TURN YOU AWAY.

YOU WILL *NEVER* BE REJECTED BY GOD. HE ALWAYS HAS OPEN ARMS, READY TO PICK YOU UP WHEN YOU ARE DOWN, AND HE'S ALWAYS READY TO LISTEN TO YOU WHEN YOU NEED SOMEONE TO TALK TO.

GOD FINDS GREAT JOY IN HIS CHILDREN AND WILL DO EVERYTHING IN HIS POWER TO ENCOURAGE THEM AND HELP THEM TO BE ALL HE HAS CREATED THEM TO BE. GOD WANTS TO SHARE THIS JOY WITH OTHERS THROUGH THE HOLY SPIRIT LIVING THROUGH YOU.

ARE *YOU* WILLING TO LET THE HOLY SPIRIT SHARE GOD'S JOY WITH OTHERS THROUGH YOU AND YOUR LIFE?

 PEACE

WHAT IS PEACE? JESUS TELLS US THAT HE LEAVES *HIS* PEACE WITH US, THAT HIS PEACE HE GIVES TO US.

HE TELLS US THAT WE SHOULD NOT LET OUR HEARTS BE TROUBLED, EVEN THOUGH IN THIS WORLD WE WILL EXPERIENCE TROUBLE.

THE OPPOSITE OF PEACE IS *WAR*. BEFORE WE CAME TO KNOW THE LORD, WE WERE AT WAR WITH HIM. YET, EVEN WHILE WE WERE GOD'S ENEMIES, CHRIST DIED FOR US!

SO NOW THAT YOU ARE A CHILD OF GOD, SHOULD YOU NOT HAVE PEACE AT ALL TIMES? IS THAT EVEN POSSIBLE? IF IT WERE POSSIBLE, IT WOULD DEPEND ON EACH PERSON'S RELATIONSHIP WITH THE LORD AND THEIR WILLINGNESS TO BELIEVE THE TRUTH.

GOD TELLS US THAT WHEN WE SEEK TO HAVE THINGS OUR OWN WAY, WE ARE LIVING IN THE FLESH. WHAT DOES THAT REALLY MEAN?

IT MEANS WE ARE LIVING BY OUR OWN WILL AND BY OUR OWN POWER—WANTING THINGS OUR OWN WAY. EVEN AS A CHILD OF GOD, WE CAN EXPERIENCE TROUBLE AND BE AT WAR IN OUR MINDS WITH GOD AND HIS WILL FOR US.

PEACE IS *NOT* THE ABSENCE OF CONFLICT. IN THE MIDST OF CONFLICT, WE CAN EXPERIENCE AN INNER STATE OF BEING THAT HELPS US STAY FOCUSED AND ASSURED IN GOD'S POWER, TRUSTING IN HIM AND HIS LOVE AND WILL FOR US.

THAT GIVES US *PEACE*!

SCRAMBLED CIRCLES

UNSCRAMBLE THE WORDS FROM THE LIST BELOW. THEN USE THE CIRCLED LETTERS ON THE NEXT PAGE TO COMPLETE THE VERSE.

1. TAORHU
2. LWROD
3. YJO
4. EBTROLU
5. NEGBI
6. MECLWEO
7. PEITS
8. WNDO

54

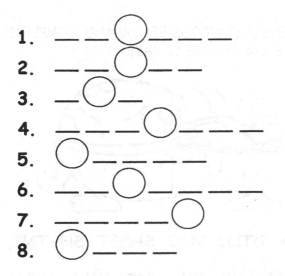

1. _ _ ◯ _ _ _
2. _ _ ◯ _ _
3. _ ◯ _
4. _ _ _ ◯ _ _ _
5. ◯ _ _ _ _
6. _ _ ◯ _ _ _
7. _ _ _ _ ◯
8. ◯ _ _ _

"PEACE I LEAVE WITH YOU; MY PEACE I GIVE YOU. I DO NOT GIVE TO YOU AS THE WORLD GIVES. DO NOT LET YOUR HEARTS BE _ _ _ _ _ _ _ AND DO NOT BE AFRAID."

JOHN 14:27

SCRAMBLED VERSES

UNSCRAMBLE THE WORDS BELOW AND COMPLETE THE VERSE ON THE NEXT PAGE.

"I VHEA DTLO YUO SHEET SHGTNI, OS THAT NI EM UYO YMA VEHA CEEAP. NI SHTI DWLRO YUO LWIL VHEA ETLRBOU. UBT KAET RHETA! I VEHA EOVOERMC ETH LWRDO."

JOHN 16:33

57

SCRAMBLED CIRCLES

UNSCRAMBLE THE WORDS FROM THE LIST BELOW. THEN USE THE CIRCLED LETTERS ON THE NEXT PAGE TO COMPLETE THE VERSE.

1. MHI

2. RCUOEGANE

3. WSEN

4. ESJUS

5. TFIAH

6. GVEI

7. MSEA

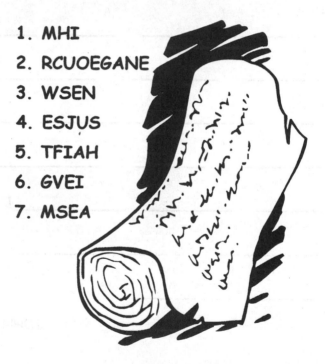

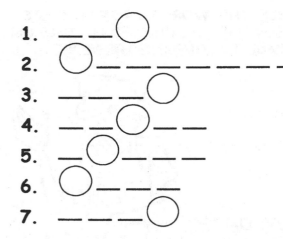

1. _ _ ◯
2. ◯ _ _ _ _ _ _ _
3. _ _ _ ◯
4. _ _ ◯ _ _
5. _ ◯ _ _ _
6. ◯ _ _ _
7. _ _ _ ◯

"YOU KNOW THE _ _ _ _ _ _ _
GOD SENT TO THE PEOPLE OF ISRAEL,
TELLING THE GOOD NEWS OF PEACE
THROUGH JESUS CHRIST, WHO IS LORD
OF ALL."

ACTS 10:36

SCRAMBLED CIRCLES

UNSCRAMBLE THE WORDS FROM THE LIST BELOW. THEN USE THE CIRCLED LETTERS ON THE NEXT PAGE TO COMPLETE THE VERSE.

1. EVROMCEO
2. RHEAT
3. LDRO
4. SOWHLELFPI
5. NSO
6. ITRHG

60

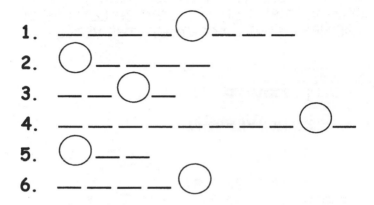

1. __ __ __ __ ◯ __ __ __
2. ◯ __ __ __ __
3. __ __ ◯ __
4. __ __ __ __ __ __ __ __ ◯ __
5. ◯ __ __
6. __ __ __ __ ◯

"GRACE AND PEACE TO YOU FROM GOD OUR FATHER AND FROM THE LORD JESUS __ __ __ __ __ __."

ROMANS 1:7

SCRAMBLED CIRCLES

UNSCRAMBLE THE WORDS FROM THE LIST BELOW. THEN USE THE CIRCLED LETTERS ON THE NEXT PAGE TO COMPLETE THE VERSE.

1. ORWEP

2. ROWLFVEO

3. LDELCA

4. HRIANCTSI

5. RVEE

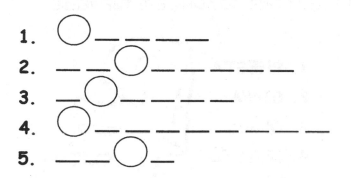

1. ◯ _ _ _ _
2. _ _ ◯ _ _ _ _ _
3. _ ◯ _ _ _ _
4. ◯ _ _ _ _ _ _ _
5. _ _ ◯ _

"THEREFORE, SINCE WE HAVE BEEN JUSTIFIED THROUGH FAITH, WE HAVE __ __ __ __ __ WITH GOD THROUGH OUR LORD JESUS CHRIST."

ROMANS 5:1

SCRAMBLED CIRCLES

UNSCRAMBLE THE WORDS FROM THE LIST BELOW. THEN USE THE CIRCLED LETTERS ON THE NEXT PAGE TO COMPLETE THE VERSE.

1. RHESTA
2. DINM
3. OLBEN
4. LFILUFL
5. DUNO
6. ELVYOL

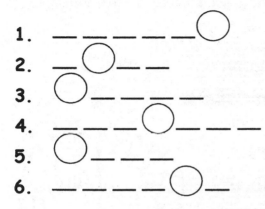

1. _ _ _ _ _◯

2. _◯_ _

3. ◯_ _ _ _

4. _ _ _◯_ _ _

5. ◯_ _ _

6. _ _ _ _◯_

"THE MIND OF _ _ _ _ _ _ MAN
IS DEATH, BUT THE MIND CONTROLLED
BY THE SPIRIT IS LIFE AND PEACE."

ROMANS 8:6

SCRAMBLED CIRCLES

UNSCRAMBLE THE WORDS FROM THE LIST BELOW. THEN USE THE CIRCLED LETTERS ON THE NEXT PAGE TO COMPLETE THE VERSE.

1. YEDN

2. BMMEESR

3. ALPCE

4. POHE

5. MDNI

6. RUADG

7. DSVEA

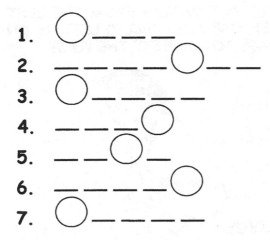

1. ◯ __ __ __ __
2. __ __ __ __ ◯ __ __
3. ◯ __ __ __ __
4. __ __ __ ◯
5. __ __ ◯ __
6. __ __ __ __ ◯
7. ◯ __ __ __ __

"IF IT IS POSSIBLE, AS FAR AS IT
__ __ __ __ __ __ __ ON YOU, LIVE AT
PEACE WITH EVERYONE."

ROMANS 12:18

67

SCRAMBLED CIRCLES

UNSCRAMBLE THE WORDS FROM THE LIST BELOW. THEN USE THE CIRCLED LETTERS ON THE NEXT PAGE TO COMPLETE THE VERSE.

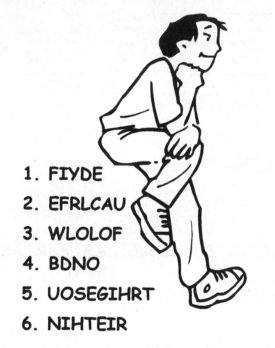

1. FIYDE

2. EFRLCAU

3. WLOLOF

4. BDNO

5. UOSEGIHRT

6. NIHTEIR

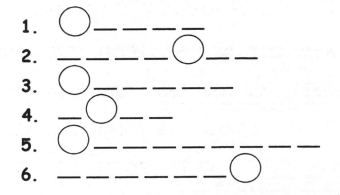

1. ◯ _ _ _ _

2. _ _ _ _ ◯ _ _

3. ◯ _ _ _ _ _

4. _ ◯ _ _

5. ◯ _ _ _ _ _ _ _

6. _ _ _ _ _ _ ◯

"LET   US   THEREFORE   MAKE   EVERY
       __ __ __ __ __ __ TO DO WHAT LEADS
TO PEACE AND TO MUTUAL EDIFICATION."

ROMANS 14:19

69

SCRAMBLED VERSES

UNSCRAMBLE THE WORDS BELOW AND COMPLETE THE VERSE ON THE NEXT PAGE.

"AYM EHT DGO FO PEOH LFIL UYO HWTI LAL YOJ DNA CEPAE SA UYO TTRUS NI MHI, OS THAT UYO YMA WOOVRELF HWTI POEH YB EHT ROWEP FO ETH YHLO RPTSII."

"_____ _____ _____ _____

_____ _____ _____

_____ _____

_____ _____ _____

_____ _____' _____

_____ _____ _____

_____ _____ _____

_____ _____ _____ _____

_____ _____ _____."

ROMANS 15:13

71

SCRAMBLED CIRCLES

UNSCRAMBLE THE WORDS FROM THE LIST BELOW. THEN USE THE CIRCLED LETTERS ON THE NEXT PAGE TO COMPLETE THE VERSE.

1. YOLH
2. OYJ
3. UELR
4. IUTSJYF
5. LTEENG
6. THARFE
7. DISOMW
8. ONHWS

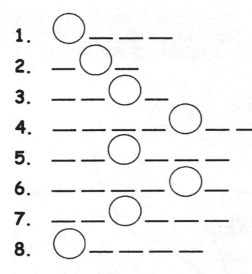

1. ⬤ __ __ __
2. __ ⬤ __
3. __ __ ⬤ __
4. __ __ __ ⬤ __ __
5. __ __ ⬤ __ __ __
6. __ __ __ ⬤ __ __
7. __ __ ⬤ __ __ __
8. ⬤ __ __ __ __

"MAKE EVERY EFFORT TO LIVE IN PEACE WITH ALL MEN AND TO BE HOLY; WITHOUT __ __ __ __ __ __ __ __ NO ONE WILL SEE THE LORD."

HEBREWS 12:14

SCRAMBLED CIRCLES

UNSCRAMBLE THE WORDS FROM THE LIST BELOW. THEN USE THE CIRCLED LETTERS ON THE NEXT PAGE TO COMPLETE THE VERSE.

1. YULFOJ

2. MDNI

3. DIGNMOK

4. RPPOTEH

5. EUYROSFL

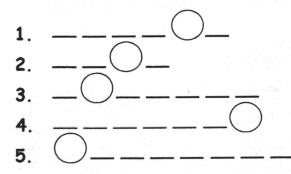

1. _ _ _ _ ⃝ _
2. _ _ ⃝ _
3. _ ⃝ _ _ _ _ _
4. _ _ _ _ _ ⃝
5. ⃝ _ _ _ _ _ _

"MAKE EVERY EFFORT TO KEEP THE
_ _ _ _ _ OF THE SPIRIT
THROUGH THE BOND OF PEACE."

EPHESIANS 4:3

SCRAMBLED CIRCLES

UNSCRAMBLE THE WORDS FROM THE LIST BELOW. THEN USE THE CIRCLED LETTERS ON THE NEXT PAGE TO COMPLETE THE VERSE.

1. FROFET
2. DLRO
3. STSNIA
4. IDKN
5. KPESA
6. VEERMOCO
7. VANEHE
8. EAMN
9. OYDB
10. EOHNCS

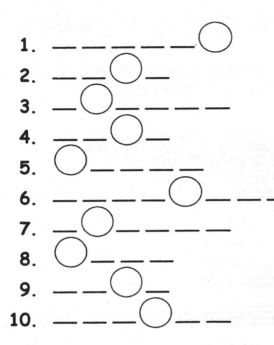

1. _ _ _ _ _ ◯
2. _ _ ◯ _
3. _ ◯ _ _ _
4. _ _ ◯ _
5. ◯ _ _ _ _
6. _ _ _ _ ◯ _ _ _
7. _ ◯ _ _ _
8. ◯ _ _ _
9. _ _ ◯ _
10. _ _ _ ◯ _ _

"AND THE PEACE OF GOD, WHICH
_ _ _ _ _ _ _ _ _ _ ALL
UNDERSTANDING, WILL GUARD YOUR
HEARTS AND YOUR MINDS IN CHRIST
JESUS."

PHILIPPIANS 4:7

SCRAMBLED VERSES

UNSCRAMBLE THE WORDS BELOW AND COMPLETE
THE VERSE ON THE NEXT PAGE.

"ELT EHT CPAEE FO TCSHRI LREU NI

RYUO RHETSA, NECIS SA SMEBMER

FO NEO DBOY UYO RWEE LAELDC OT

CEAPE. NDA EB NFULTAHK."

"_____

____ ____ ____ ____ ____ ____

____ ____ ____ ____ ____

____ ____ _____, ____

____ ____ ____ ____ ____

____ ____ ____ ____ ____

____ ____ ____ ____ ____.

____ ____ ____ ____."

____ ____ _____."

COLOSSIANS 3:15

SCRAMBLED CIRCLES

UNSCRAMBLE THE WORDS FROM THE LIST BELOW. THEN USE THE CIRCLED LETTERS ON THE NEXT PAGE TO COMPLETE THE VERSE.

1. TERAH
2. CTPAEENI
3. RSEIMPO
4. NHTASK
5. OERTW
6. OAILSTVAN
7. LILF

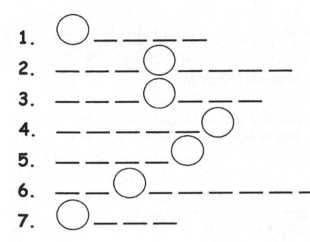

1. ○ __ __ __ __
2. __ __ __ ○ __ __ __ __
3. __ __ __ ○ __ __ __
4. __ __ __ __ ○
5. __ __ __ __ ○
6. __ __ ○ __ __ __ __ __
7. ○ __ __ __

"NOW MAY THE LORD OF PEACE
__ __ __ __ __ __ __ GIVE YOU PEACE
AT ALL TIMES AND IN EVERY WAY. THE
LORD BE WITH ALL OF YOU."

2 THESSALONIANS 3:16

81

THINK, THINK, THINK

PEACE IS WHAT YOU RECEIVE WHEN YOU ACCEPT GOD'S INVITATION—PEACE IN YOUR HEART AND IN YOUR MIND.

JESUS CAME TO BRING US PEACE—THE KIND OF PEACE THAT MAKES IT POSSIBLE FOR US TO *"TAKE HEART"* AND HAVE COURAGE WHEN WE ARE EXPERIENCING STRUGGLES. THE PEACE GOD GIVES US THROUGH HIS HOLY SPIRIT IS A PEACE BEYOND HUMAN UNDERSTANDING.

BY ACCEPTING GOD'S INVITATION AND PUTTING YOUR FAITH IN JESUS CHRIST AND WHAT HE HAS DONE FOR YOU, YOU WILL ALWAYS BE AT PEACE WITH GOD.

YOU MAY NOT ALWAYS BE AT PEACE WITH YOURSELF, AND WHEN THAT HAPPENS, YOU HAVE A CHOICE TO TURN TO GOD FOR HELP AND GUIDANCE OR TO STAY IN YOUR FEELINGS AND STRUGGLES.

GOD GIVES YOU THE ABILITY TO LIVE A LIFE *ABOVE* YOUR FEELINGS AND CIRCUMSTANCES, BUT THIS CANNOT BE DONE BY YOUR OWN WILLPOWER AND STRENGTH. YOU NEED TO DEPEND ON THE LORD FOR THIS. HE WILL GIVE YOU THE STRENGTH, POWER, AND PEACE TO LIVE ABOVE ALL THINGS.

THERE IS NOTHING GOD IS NOT WILLING TO HELP YOU WITH, AND WHEN YOU DEPEND ON GOD, YOU WILL EXPERIENCE HIS PEACE THROUGH HIS HOLY SPIRIT.

ARE YOU DEPENDING ON THE LORD TO HELP YOU OR ARE YOU DEPENDING ON YOURSELF? WHAT DOES GOD WANT YOU TO DO?

PATIENCE

WHAT IS PATIENCE? ANYONE CAN BE PATIENT WHEN EVERYTHING IS GOING WELL AND TO HIS LIKING, BUT THE TRUE TEST OF PATIENCE IS WHEN *EVERYTHING IS GOING WRONG*!

HOW DO YOU REACT WHEN NOTHING SEEMS TO BE GOING RIGHT? DO YOU BECOME ANGRY AND IRRITABLE? DO YOU TRY TO FORCE A SOLUTION BY CONTROLLING EVERYTHING?

DO YOU THINK YOU BECOME IMPATIENT AND IRRITABLE BECAUSE YOU ARE DEPENDING ON *YOURSELF* TO GET THROUGH SUCH TIMES? WHEN THINGS GO WRONG, INSTEAD OF TRYING TO WORK EVERYTHING OUT YOURSELF, WHY NOT TRY TURNING TO GOD FOR HIS HELP?

GOD KNOWS WHAT IS GOING TO HAPPEN. HE HAS A SOLUTION FOR EVERY PROBLEM.

MANY OF US THINK THAT WHEN WE ASK GOD FOR HELP, THE SOLUTION SHOULD COME RIGHT AWAY. SOMETIMES IT DOES—AND SOMETIMES IT DOESN'T.

WHEN IT *DOESN'T* IS WHEN WE REALLY NEED PATIENCE; THIS IS WHEN WE REALLY NEED TO TURN TO GOD AND DEPEND ON HIM. LEARNING TO WAIT IS NOT EASY. WE CAN'T ALWAYS HAVE WHAT WE WANT WHEN WE WANT IT.

WE CAN TRUST THAT GOD IS WORKING EVERYTHING OUT FOR GOOD. WE CAN TRUST EVERYTHING IS ON SCHEDULE AND THINGS ARE BEING WORKED OUT. THE SOLUTION AND ANSWERS WILL COME.

WAITING TIME IS NOT WASTED TIME.

SCRAMBLED VERSES

UNSCRAMBLE THE WORDS BELOW AND COMPLETE THE VERSE ON THE NEXT PAGE.

"RTEHEROFE, SA D'GOS NCEHSO LPEEOP,

YHLO DNA RDYLAE DLVOE, ELHCOT

SSEVROUYLE HWTI NMCOSASPOI,

SDKSENIN, TLYIIUMH, SGSENELTNE

DAN EPCANTEI."

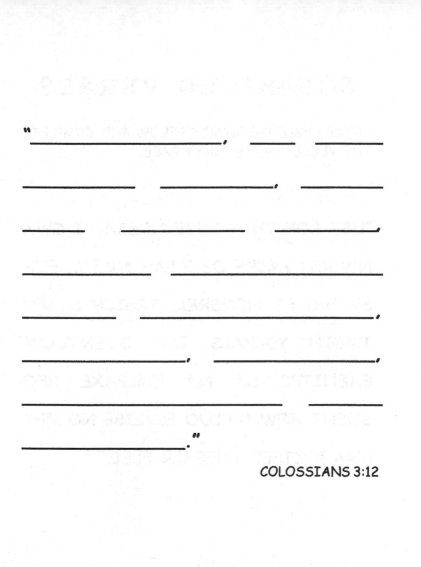

"_____, _____ _____

_____ _____, _____

_____ _____ _____,

_____ _____

_____ _____,

_____, _____,

_____ _____

_____."

COLOSSIANS 3:12

SCRAMBLED VERSES

UNSCRAMBLE THE WORDS BELOW AND COMPLETE
THE VERSE ON THE NEXT PAGE.

"UBT ROF THAT RVYE NRESAO I SWA

NWSOH YMCRE OS TTAH NI EM, ETH

SWTRO FO NSNSREI, TRSICH SJSEU

TMGIH YDLPAIS ISH DUENTLIIM

EAENITPC SA NA EMLPAXE RFO

SOEHT HOW DWLUO ELVEIBE NO MHI

DNA RVCIEEE TNEEALR FLEI."

1 TIMOTHY 1:16

SCRAMBLED VERSES

UNSCRAMBLE THE WORDS BELOW AND COMPLETE
THE VERSE ON THE NEXT PAGE.

"CPHRAE HET DORW; EB DRAEPPER

NI SNESOA DAN UOT FO SNESAO;

RCCTEOR, ERKEUB DAN GEENACRUO—

HWTI TGERA EPCANTIE DAN LCFREUA

NINOITSTURC."

2 TIMOTHY 4:2

SCRAMBLED CIRCLES

UNSCRAMBLE THE WORDS FROM THE LIST
BELOW. THEN USE THE CIRCLED LETTERS ON
THE NEXT PAGE TO COMPLETE THE VERSE.

1. UIITYLMH

2. NCVIONCE

3. RGHTNTES

4. ERPETN

5. NSRTE

6. IDLHC

7. GHITL

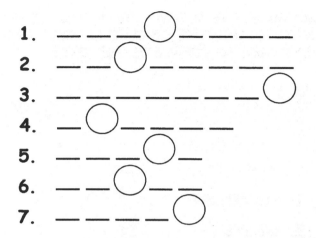

1. _ _ _ ◯ _ _ _ _
2. _ _ ◯ _ _ _ _ _
3. _ _ _ _ _ _ _ ◯
4. _ ◯ _ _ _ _ _
5. _ _ _ ◯ _
6. _ _ ◯ _ _
7. _ _ _ ◯ _

"WE DO NOT WANT YOU TO BECOME
LAZY, BUT TO IMITATE THOSE
WHO THROUGH FAITH AND PATIENCE
__ __ __ __ __ __ __ WHAT HAS BEEN
PROMISED."

HEBREWS 6:12

SCRAMBLED CIRCLES

UNSCRAMBLE THE WORDS FROM THE LIST BELOW. THEN USE THE CIRCLED LETTERS ON THE NEXT PAGE TO COMPLETE THE VERSE.

1. ALSESEP

2. IDOVDRPE

3. LODYG

4. LEWONDEGK

5. IDIVEN

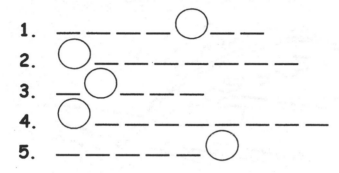

1. _ _ _ _ ◯ _ _
2. ◯ _ _ _ _ _ _ _
3. _ ◯ _ _ _
4. ◯ _ _ _ _ _ _ _
5. _ _ _ _ _ ◯

"BROTHERS, AS AN EXAMPLE OF PATIENCE IN THE FACE OF SUFFERING, TAKE THE PROPHETS WHO _ _ _ _ _ IN THE NAME OF THE LORD."

JAMES 5:10

95

SCRAMBLED VERSES

UNSCRAMBLE THE WORDS BELOW AND COMPLETE
THE VERSE ON THE NEXT PAGE.

"REBA NI NDIM THAT ROU RLDO'S

ETCANPEI SMNAE NSOAILTVA, SJTU

SA RUO READ RREHTOB LAPU SALO

ERTWO UOY HWTI ETH MSODIW

THAT DGO EGAV MHI."

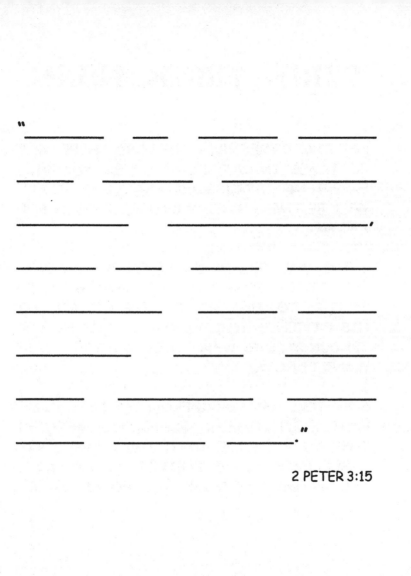

"

＿＿＿＿＿＿ ＿＿＿ ＿＿＿ ＿＿＿＿

＿＿＿＿ ＿＿＿＿ ＿＿＿ ＿＿＿＿＿

＿＿＿＿＿ ＿＿＿＿＿＿＿＿,

＿＿＿＿ ＿＿＿ ＿＿＿ ＿＿＿＿

＿＿＿＿ ＿＿ ＿＿＿

＿＿＿＿ ＿＿ ＿＿＿

＿＿＿ ＿＿＿ ＿＿＿＿

＿＿＿ ＿＿＿ ＿＿＿."

2 PETER 3:15

97

THINK, THINK, THINK

PATIENCE COMES FROM THE LORD. THERE WILL BE TIMES IN OUR LIVES WHEN WE WILL EXPERIENCE STRUGGLES AND LOSS. THERE WILL BE TIMES WHEN WE HAVE TO WAIT FOR ANSWERS.

THERE WILL BE TIMES WHEN WE DO NOT WANT TO WAIT, AND THAT IS WHEN WE *NEED* TO TURN TO THE LORD FOR HELP AND ASK FOR HIS PATIENCE TO LIVE IN US. OUR HUMAN TENDENCY IS TO WANT WHAT WE WANT AND WANT IT NOW.

SOMETIMES ANSWERS FROM THE LORD COME FAST, EVEN IMMEDIATELY—BUT SOMETIMES THEY DO NOT COME RIGHT AWAY. THERE ARE *THREE ANSWERS* WE RECEIVE FROM GOD WHEN ASKING FOR SOMETHING: YES, NO, OR WAIT.

IT'S GREAT WHEN GOD'S ANSWER IS *YES*, BUT WHEN HE TELLS YOU *NO*, IT WILL TAKE TIME AND PRAYER TO HELP YOU ACCEPT HIS ANSWER. ONE THING TO REMEMBER IS THAT WHEN GOD SAYS NO, HE HAS HIS REASONS, FOR HE ALONE KNOWS WHAT TOMORROW HOLDS.

THE REALLY HARD ANSWER IS *WAIT*, AS LIKE MOST OF US, YOU MAY TEND TO WANT INSTANT RESULTS. THIS IS WHEN YOU NEED TO TURN TO GOD FOR HIS PATIENCE AND HELP.

GOD WILL ALWAYS BE PATIENT WITH YOU IN YOUR STRUGGLE TO ACCEPT HIS WILL. HE IS ALWAYS WILLING TO GIVE YOU *HIS* PATIENCE THROUGH HIS HOLY SPIRIT.

IS THERE SOMETHING YOU NEED TO BE PATIENT ABOUT? HAVE YOU ASKED GOD FOR HIS PATIENCE AND HELP?

KINDNESS

WHAT IS KINDNESS? IT MEANS TO BE TOLERANT, HELPFUL, SINCERE, SUPPORTIVE, ENCOURAGING, CONSIDERATE, NICE, AND GENEROUS.

GOD IS ALL THESE THINGS WITH US. HE IS ALWAYS TREATING US WITH *LOVING* KINDNESS.

HE IS CONSIDERATE OF US AND IS ALWAYS GENEROUS TO US AND WILLING TO HELP US. HE IS SINCERE WHEN HE SAYS HE LOVES US AND IN EVERYTHING HE DOES AND GIVES. HE IS FOREVER THERE TO ENCOURAGE US TO BE THE BEST WE CAN BE. HE IS ALWAYS UNDERSTANDING AND COMPASSIONATE OF OUR NEEDS AND LIMITATIONS.

GOD IS TENDER AND LOVING WITH ALL OF HIS CHILDREN AND IS SUPPORTIVE IN HELPING US TO LEARN ABOUT HIM.

HE IS ALWAYS WILLING TO SHOW YOU THE TRUTH AND REVEAL TO YOU HIS LOVE AND JUST HOW MUCH HE BELIEVES IN YOU!

AS YOU LEARN AND BEGIN TO EXPERIENCE GOD'S KINDNESS TO YOU, DON'T YOU WANT TO SHOW MORE KINDNESS TO OTHERS?

SCRAMBLED CIRCLES

UNSCRAMBLE THE WORDS FROM THE LIST BELOW. THEN USE THE CIRCLED LETTERS ON THE NEXT PAGE TO COMPLETE THE VERSE.

1. INKNGOW

2. PAENCEIT

3. BNOR

4. WDON

5. LDRHECIN

6. ACEPE

7. RAIPSE

8. RITSPI

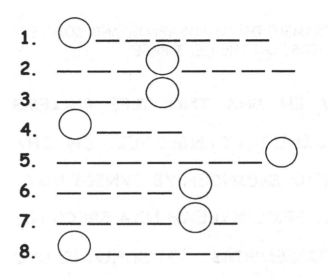

1. ◯ _ _ _ _ _ _
2. _ _ ◯ _ _ _ _ _
3. _ _ ◯ _ _ _ _
4. ◯ _ _ _
5. _ _ _ _ _ _ _ ◯
6. _ _ _ ◯
7. _ _ _ ◯ _
8. ◯ _ _ _ _ _

"'I HAVE LOVED YOU WITH AN EVER-LASTING LOVE; I HAVE DRAWN YOU WITH LOVING-__ __ __ __ __ __ __ __.'"

JEREMIAH 31:3

103

SCRAMBLED VERSES

UNSCRAMBLE THE WORDS BELOW AND COMPLETE
THE VERSE ON THE NEXT PAGE.

"ETY EH SHA TNO TLFE FHLIEMS

TWOIHUT YTTNMOSEI: EH SHA

NSWHO SKDINSEN YB GVNIGI UOY

NRIA RFMO NVEEAH NDA SRPCO NI

RHETI SENSOAS; EH SDPRVOEI UYO

HWIT YPTLNE FO ODOF DAN SLILF

RUYO SETARH TIHW OJY."

ACTS 14:17

105

SCRAMBLED CIRCLES

UNSCRAMBLE THE WORDS FROM THE LIST BELOW. THEN USE THE CIRCLED LETTERS ON THE NEXT PAGE TO COMPLETE THE VERSE.

1. DOLR

2. TIHAF

3. DNSESNIK

4. WEENRLA

5. IHRTB

6. EDEN

7. DOGO

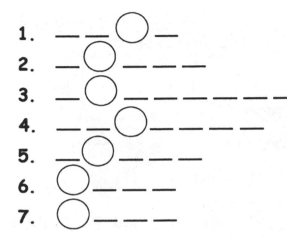

1. _ _ ◯ _
2. _ ◯ _ _ _
3. _ ◯ _ _ _ _ _
4. _ _ ◯ _ _ _ _
5. _ ◯ _ _ _
6. ◯ _ _ _
7. ◯ _ _ _

"THE ISLANDERS SHOWED US UNUSUAL KINDNESS. THEY BUILT A FIRE AND WELCOMED US ALL BECAUSE IT WAS _ _ _ _ _ _ _ AND COLD."

ACTS 28:2

SCRAMBLED VERSES

UNSCRAMBLE THE WORDS BELOW AND COMPLETE
THE VERSE ON THE NEXT PAGE.

"RO OD UYO WHSO TTMPENCO FRO

EHT SRHECI FO SHI SKSENNID,

EAEOLTRNC DAN EPACNTEI, ONT

GRNEAILZI TTAH D'SOG SISKENND

ESDAL OUY DWTAOR EPECRNANET?"

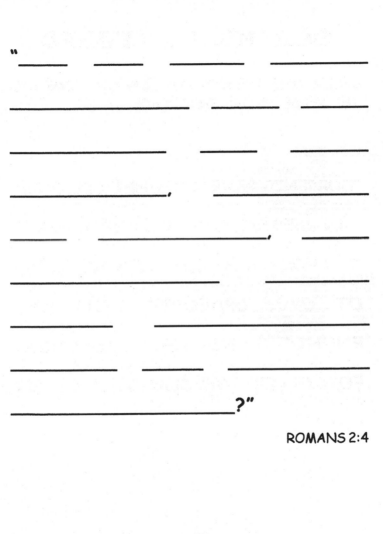

"_____ _____ _____ _____ _____
_____ _____ _____
_____ _____ _____ _____
_____, _____
_____ _____, _____
_____ _____
_____ _____
_____ _____ _____
_____?"

ROMANS 2:4

SCRAMBLED VERSES

UNSCRAMBLE THE WORDS BELOW AND COMPLETE
THE VERSE ON THE NEXT PAGE.

"DORCENIS EEHRTORFE HET SKISENDN
DAN RSESTSENN FO DGO: SNTNSERES
OT EHOST WOH ELLF, UTB SKSINEND
OT OYU, DPDEORIV TTHA UYO
ENUNICTO NI HSI SISKENDN.
EOTSIHWER, UYO SLAO ILWL BE UCT
FOF."

"_____ _____
_____ _____ ___
_____ ___ ___ _____:
_____ ___ _____
_____ _____, _____
_____ ___ _____,
_____ ___ _____
_____ ___ _____
_____. _____,
___ _____ ___ ___ ___
___ _____."

ROMANS 11:22

111

SCRAMBLED VERSES

UNSCRAMBLE THE WORDS BELOW AND COMPLETE
THE VERSE ON THE NEXT PAGE.

"UTB NWHE EHT SKISENND DAN ELVO

FO DGO ROU RSIOAV PEDAPREA, EH

DSVEA SU, ONT ESUACBE FO

SRIOUGHET STHGNI EW DHA EDNO,

UBT EBESUCA FO IHS YMCRE. EH

DSAEV US HTHGRUO ETH GWSHIAN

FO HRETRBI DAN LREAWNE YB EHT

YOLH RPITIS."

"_____ _____ _____
_____ _____ _____
____ ____ ____ _____
_____, ____ _____
____, _____ _____
____ _____ _____
_____ _____ ____, ____
_____ ____ ____
_____. ____ _____
____ _____ _____
_____ ____ ____ _____
____ _____ _____
____ _____ _____."

TITUS 3:4–5

THINK, THINK, THINK

GOD IS ALWAYS KIND AND IS FOREVER TRYING TO DRAW US CLOSER TO HIM THROUGH HIS LOVING-KINDNESS.

THERE WILL BE MANY TIMES IN YOUR LIFE WHEN YOU WILL NEED TO BE KIND TO THOSE WHO ARE NOT KIND TO YOU. THERE WILL BE TIMES WHEN PEOPLE DO WRONG TOWARD YOU AND ARE MEAN TO YOU, AND YOU WILL REPAY THEIR UNKINDNESS WITH KINDNESS.

HOW DO YOU DO THAT?

IT IS HUMAN TO WANT TO TREAT THOSE WHO TREAT YOU UNKINDLY IN THE SAME WAY, BUT WHAT GOD ASKS OF US IS NOT TO REPAY EVIL WITH EVIL BUT TO REPAY EVIL WITH GOOD.

BEFORE WE BECAME GOD'S CHILDREN, HE SHOWED HIS KINDNESS TO US IN MANY WAYS. EVEN THOUGH WE WANTED NOTHING TO DO WITH GOD, HE NEVER GAVE UP ON US. HE SENT HIS PEOPLE ACROSS OUR PATHS TO TELL US ABOUT HIS LOVE AND WHY HE SENT HIS ONE AND ONLY SON TO DIE FOR US.

IF GOD WAS KIND TO US WHILE WE WERE BEING UNKIND TO HIM, HOW MUCH MORE WILL HE BE KIND *THROUGH* YOU TO THOSE WHO ARE NOT SO KIND TO YOU?

ARE YOU WILLING TO ASK GOD TO PUT HIS KINDNESS IN YOUR HEART FOR SOME PERSON WHO MAY HAVE TREATED YOU WRONG? HOW DO YOU THINK THAT WILL CHANGE THINGS?

GOODNESS

WHAT IS GOODNESS? GOODNESS MEANS TO BE FAIR, HONEST, GIVING, KIND, DECENT, TRUSTWORTHY, AND RELIABLE.

IT ALSO MEANS THAT THOSE AROUND YOU ARE *SAFE* WITH YOU. NO ONE CAN HAVE ALL OF THESE QUALITIES ALL OF THE TIME EXCEPT GOD HIMSELF.

THIS IS HOW GOD TREATS YOU. GOD IS ALWAYS FAIR AND DOES NOT HAVE FAVORITES. HE LOVES EVERYONE EQUALLY AND GIVES TO EVERYONE EQUALLY. GOD IS ALWAYS HONEST WITH YOU AND WILL ALWAYS TREAT YOU WITH COMPASSION AND KINDESS.

GOD IS ALWAYS TRUSTWORTHY, AND YOU CAN ALWAYS RELY ON HIM, NO MATTER WHAT YOU ARE THINKING, FEELING, OR GOING THROUGH.

GOD KNOWS ALL THINGS, AND THERE IS NOTHING YOU CAN HIDE FROM GOD. GOD WILL *NOT* PUNISH YOU. YOU ARE ALWAYS SAFE WITH GOD AND CAN ALWAYS BE HONEST WITH HIM.

GOD IS GOOD AND HE GIVES HIS GOODNESS TO YOU FREELY. IT'S NOT THAT YOU DO ANYTHING TO DESERVE HIS GOODNESS—HE GIVES BECAUSE OF *WHO HE IS*.

SCRAMBLED CIRCLES

UNSCRAMBLE THE WORDS FROM THE LIST BELOW. THEN USE THE CIRCLED LETTERS ON THE NEXT PAGE TO COMPLETE THE VERSE.

1. LODC
2. HILTG
3. ELOV
4. OTSCSNI
5. ASERNO
6. DGO

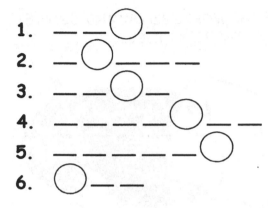

1. __ __ ◯ __
2. __ ◯ __ __ __
3. __ __ ◯ __
4. __ __ __ __ ◯ __ __
5. __ __ __ __ __ ◯
6. ◯ __ __

"I AM STILL CONFIDENT OF THIS: I WILL SEE THE GOODNESS OF THE LORD IN THE LAND OF THE __ __ __ __ __ __."

PSALM 27:13

SCRAMBLED VERSES

UNSCRAMBLE THE WORDS BELOW AND COMPLETE
THE VERSE ON THE NEXT PAGE.

"I FMYLES MA DCOECNVNI, YM

BSRROEHT, TTAH OUY SSYOEVULRE

REA LFLU FO SGOSEODN, MECTOEPL

NI EKNGDOWLE DNA TCNETEPMO OT

TTSCRUNI NEO RAENOHT."

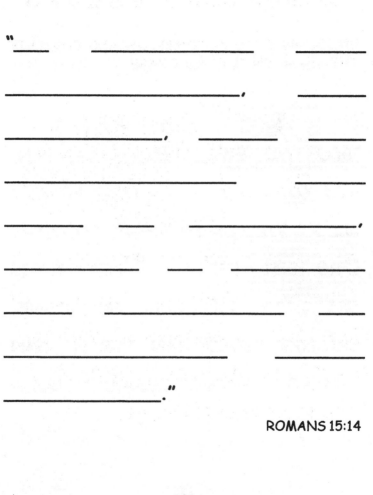

ROMANS 15:14

SCRAMBLED VERSES

UNSCRAMBLE THE WORDS BELOW AND COMPLETE
THE VERSE ON THE NEXT PAGE.

"RFO UYO EWRE EOCN SDASERKN,
BTU OWN UYO ERA LTIHG NI EHT
RLDO. VILE SA NCHLEDRI FO GLIHT
(FRO EHT TFIRU FO HET TLIHG
SSITSNCO NI LAL SGODOSNE,
SRISEGNHTSUEO DAN TURTH) DAN
DINF UTO THWA SPLEESA EHT LDOR."

"_____ _____ _____ _____
_____, _____ _____
_____ _____ _____ _____
_____ _____. _____ _____
_____ _____ _____
(____ ____ ____ ____ ____
____ ____ ____ ____
____ ____ _____,
_____ ____
____) __ ___ __ ___
__ _____ ____ ___
____."

EPHESIANS 5:8–10

SCRAMBLED VERSES

UNSCRAMBLE THE WORDS BELOW AND COMPLETE
THE VERSE ON THE NEXT PAGE.

"RFO STIH YVRE NROEAS, EKMA
REVEY FTEFRO OT DAD OT RUOY
TFIAH DOGOSNES DAN OT
OGDNOESS, ENGKDOWEL DAN OT
LKDGEEOWN ESFL-ROCNOLT ADN OT
EFLS-OCRNTLO, VSERERERPNACE; ADN
OT EPECNRASREEV, SDLGSEOIN DNA
OT LDSSOGENI, YBRLROTEH SKISNEDN
DNA OT HROTBREYL SKIDNSNE,
VLEO."

2 PETER 1:5–7

THINK, THINK, THINK

GOD'S GOODNESS REACHES THE UNREACHABLE.

GOD IS FOREVER TREATING US WITH FAIRNESS IN EVERYTHING AND SHOWS NO FAVORITISM. THERE WILL BE MANY TIMES IN YOUR LIFE WHEN YOU WILL HAVE A HARD TIME BEING GOOD TO OTHERS. THERE WILL BE TIMES WHEN YOU SHOW FAVORITISM, OR ARE DISHONEST. THERE WILL BE TIMES WHEN YOU DO NOT WANT TO GIVE TO OTHERS, WANTING ONLY FOR YOURSELF!

EVERYONE GOES THROUGH THESE TIMES OF SELFISHNESS, WHERE THEY ARE NOT RELIABLE OR TRUSTWORTHY. AS CHILDREN OF GOD, WE HAVE BEEN ASKED TO LIVE IN A *DIFFERENT* WAY.

GOD HAS GIVEN YOU HIS HOLY SPIRIT TO HELP YOU LIVE A LIFE FILLED WITH GOODNESS THAT YOU CAN SHARE WITH OTHERS.

THIS IS NOT AT ALL EASY TO DO, NOR IS IT SOMETHING GOD HAS ASKED YOU TO DO BY YOUR OWN WILLPOWER AND STRENGTH. WHEN YOU PUT YOUR TRUST IN GOD AND FOCUS ON HIM, HE WILL LIVE OUT *HIS* GOODNESS IN YOUR LIFE THROUGH THE HOLY SPIRIT.

GOD KNOWS WE ARE ONLY HUMAN, AND HE IS MORE THAN WILLING TO HELP US IN OUR WEAKNESS. IT'S WHEN WE ARE WEAK AND ADMIT TO GOD OUR WEAKNESS THAT HE IS STRONG *IN* US AND *THROUGH* US.

ARE YOU ADMITTING YOUR WEAKNESS TO GOD AND ASKING FOR HIS HELP?

FAITHFULNESS

WHAT IS FAITHFULNESS? FAITHFULNESS IS REVEALED IN ONE BEING SINCERE, LOYAL, DEVOTED, DEPENDABLE, AND BELIEVEABLE.

GOD IS ALL OF THESE THINGS. HE IS ALWAYS SINCERE IN *EVERYTHING* HE SAYS AND DOES. GOD WILL NOT LIE TO YOU. HE WILL ALWAYS BE LOYAL TO YOU, HIS CHILD, AND HE WILL NEVER LEAVE YOU OR ABANDON YOU.

HE IS ALWAYS DEVOTED TO YOU. HE WILL DO WHAT IS BEST FOR YOU AND HELP YOU BE THE BEST YOU CAN BE. HE IS NEVER-CHANGING AND WILL ALWAYS BE YOUR FREIND. WHAT HE SAYS TODAY WILL BE THE SAME TOMMORROW—NO MATTER WHAT. YOU CAN DEPEND ON GOD *ALWAYS*.

HE WILL NEVER MAKE FALSE PROMISES TO
YOU. GOD ALWAYS KEEPS HIS WORD AND
IS ALWAYS FAITHFUL IN EVERYTHING, NOT
JUST SOME THINGS.

ALL GOD WANTS FROM US IS THAT WE TRUST
HIM AND RELY ON HIM IN ALL THINGS.

LEARNING OF HIS FAITHFULNESS WILL HELP
TEACH US TO BE MORE FAITHFUL WITH OTHERS.

SCRAMBLED VERSES

UNSCRAMBLE THE WORDS BELOW AND COMPLETE THE VERSE ON THE NEXT PAGE.

"IT SI DOGO OT EPSRIA ETH ROLD DNA KMEA USMCI OT RUYO MANE, O SMOT GIHH, OT MPRIAOLC RYUO OVLE NI HET GMONIRN DNA RUYO SFASEINTLHUF TA GNHIT, OT ETH SCIMU FO ETH NTE-SDTERGNI LEYR DNA ETH YMEDOL FO EHT RPAH."

PSALM 92:1–3

131

SCRAMBLED CIRCLES

UNSCRAMBLE THE WORDS FROM THE LIST
BELOW. THEN USE THE CIRCLED LETTERS ON
THE NEXT PAGE TO COMPLETE THE VERSE.

1. ELEF

2. HTRBORE

3. ETRGA

4. TLOCEH

5. DVLEO

6. EUDESNR

7. SCHTIR

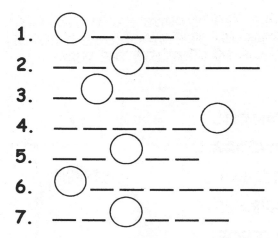

1. ◯ __ __ __
2. __ __ ◯ __ __ __ __
3. __ ◯ __ __ __ __
4. __ __ __ __ __ ◯
5. __ __ ◯ __ __
6. ◯ __ __ __ __ __ __
7. __ __ ◯ __ __ __

"FOR THE LORD IS GOOD AND HIS LOVE ENDURES __ __ __ __ __ __ __; HIS FAITHFULNESS CONTINUES THROUGH ALL GENERATIONS."

PSALM 100:5

SCRAMBLED CIRCLES

UNSCRAMBLE THE WORDS FROM THE LIST BELOW. THEN USE THE CIRCLED LETTERS ON THE NEXT PAGE TO COMPLETE THE VERSE.

1. UHTTR
2. LYEDRA
3. IDNB
4. LPPAAE
5. LPEPOE
6. LMUHIIYT

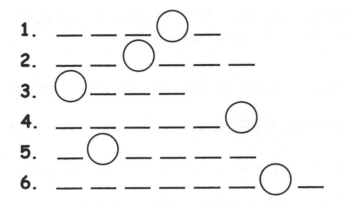

1. __ __ __ ◯ __
2. __ __ ◯ __ __ __
3. ◯ __ __ __
4. __ __ __ __ ◯
5. __ ◯ __ __ __ __
6. __ __ __ __ __ __ ◯ __

"LET LOVE AND FAITHFULNESS NEVER LEAVE
YOU; BIND THEM AROUND YOUR NECK, WRITE
THEM ON THE __ __ __ __ __ __
OF YOUR HEART."

PROVERBS 3:3

SCRAMBLED VERSES

UNSCRAMBLE THE WORDS BELOW AND COMPLETE THE VERSE ON THE NEXT PAGE.

"'RFO I, ETH RLOD, VLOE EJUCIST; I TAHE BRRYEOB NDA YITNIIUQ. NI YM SFASEINTLHUF I ILWL DRREAW MTEH DNA KMAE NA GENVEIRTSLA TCNOVENA IHTW MTHE.'"

ISAIAH 61:8

137

SCRAMBLED VERSES

UNSCRAMBLE THE WORDS BELOW AND COMPLETE THE VERSE ON THE NEXT PAGE.

"HTWA FI OSME IDD ONT VHAE

AHTIF? ILWL ERIHT CLAK FO FTAHI

YNULFIL G'DSO SFASEINTLHUF? ONT

TA LAL! ELT DGO EB RUTE, DNA

REVEY NMA A AILR."

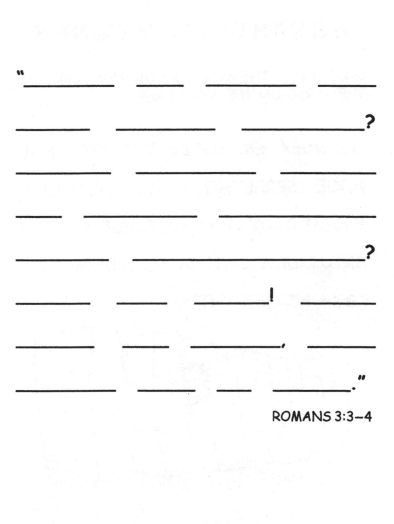

"_____ ____ ____ ____

_____ ____ _____?

_____ _____ ____

____ _____ ____

_____ _____?

____ ____ ____! ____

____ ____ ____, ____

_____ ____ ___ ____."

ROMANS 3:3–4

SCRAMBLED VERSES

UNSCRAMBLE THE WORDS BELOW AND COMPLETE
THE VERSE ON THE NEXT PAGE.

"TI VGEA EM TGRAE YJO OT VHAE

MSOE SBRRETHO OMCE DAN LTEL

TAUBO ROUY SFASEINTLHUF OT ETH

HRTUT DNA OWH OUY ECUONNIT OT

LWKA NI HET THTRU."

140

3 JOHN 1:3

THINK, THINK, THINK

GOD WILL ALWAYS BE FAITHFUL TO US IN ALL THINGS. HE ALWAYS KEEPS HIS WORD AND HIS TRUTH NEVER CHANGES.

GOD WILL ALWAYS BE DEVOTED TO YOU, HIS CHILD. HE WILL ALWAYS WORK IN YOU AND WITH YOU. HIS FAITHFULNESS TO YOU DOES *NOT* DEPEND ON YOUR FAITHFULNESS TO HIM.

WHEN GOD TELLS YOU HE WILL ALWAYS BE THERE FOR YOU, YOU CAN TRUST HIM AT HIS WORD. YOUR LACK OF FAITH DOES NOT STOP GOD'S FAITHFULNESS, NOR IS HE LIKE PEOPLE WHO DON'T KEEP THEIR PROMISES. GOD ALWAYS DOES WHAT HE PROMISES AND *NEVER* WILL HE LIE TO YOU.

THERE WILL BE MANY TIMES IN YOUR LIFE THAT YOU WILL BE ASKED TO BE A PERSON OF YOUR WORD AND TO BE DEVOTED TO OTHERS— TO DO WHAT YOU SAY YOU WILL DO. THERE WILL BE MANY TIMES THAT YOU WILL BE ASKED TO BE LOYAL AND TRUSTWORTHY.

THERE WILL ALSO BE MANY TIMES YOU WILL FALL SHORT IN ALL THESE THINGS. HUMANS *USUALLY* FALL SHORT, BUT GOD NEVER DOES.

WHEN WE PUT OUR DEPENDENCE ON GOD, HIS FAITHFULNESS WILL LIVE THROUGH US AND REACH OTHERS IN OUR LIVES.

ARE YOU BEING ASKED TO BE FAITHFUL? ARE YOU HAVING A HARD TIME DOING THIS? ARE YOU WILLING TO ASK GOD TO BE FAITHFUL *THROUGH* YOU?

GENTLENESS

WHAT IS GENTLENESS? IT MEANS BEING FRIENDLY, KIND-HEARTED, PLEASANT, TENDER, SENSITIVE, COMPASSIONATE, LIKABLE, CALM, AND GRACIOUS.

SO MANY TIMES WE COMPARE GOD TO OUR EXPERIENCES WITH OTHER PEOPLE. GOD IS *NOT* LIKE OTHER PEOPLE. HE IS ALWAYS GENTLE AND CARING, NEVER HARSH. HE IS FRIENDLY AND APPROACHABLE. THE LORD IS SENSITIVE TO YOUR NEEDS AND HAS COMPASSION FOR YOU.

HE IS ALWAYS CALM AND GRACIOUS WITH YOU, TENDER IN EVERYTHING HE DOES. GOD COMPLETELY UNDERSTANDS YOU AND WHAT YOU ARE GOING THROUGH. WHEN YOU DO THINGS WRONG, GOD WILL *NOT* TURN AWAY FROM YOU BUT WILL HELP YOU MAKE YOUR WRONGS INTO RIGHTS.

WHEN YOU ARE STRUGGLING WITH THINGS, GOD IS THERE TO LISTEN TO YOU AND HELP YOU IN ANY WAY HE CAN.

GOD WILL NEVER DO ANYTHING TO HARM YOU IN ANY WAY. GOD IS ALWAYS THERE WITH OPEN ARMS, INVITING YOU TO COME TO HIM.

WOULD YOU LIKE TO BE AS GENTLE WITH OTHERS AS GOD IS WITH YOU?

SCRAMBLED VERSES

UNSCRAMBLE THE WORDS BELOW AND COMPLETE
THE VERSE ON THE NEXT PAGE.

"YB HET SMSEEEKN DNA SGESENTNEL

FO SCTRHI, I LAPAPE OT UOY—I,

UPAL, HOW MA 'MTIDI' ENHW CFAE

OT CAFE ITWH OYU, UTB 'LDBO'

HENW WYAA!"

146

2 CORINTHIANS 10:1

SCRAMBLED VERSES

UNSCRAMBLE THE WORDS BELOW AND COMPLETE THE VERSE ON THE NEXT PAGE.

"EREREOFHT, SA G'SOD SCNHOE EPOPEL, LYHO DNA RDLEYA VLEOD, CELHOT SYEOVULRES IWTH SCONMAPSOI, KNSESNID, IHLUMIYT, TSSENGELEN DNA ATPEINEC."

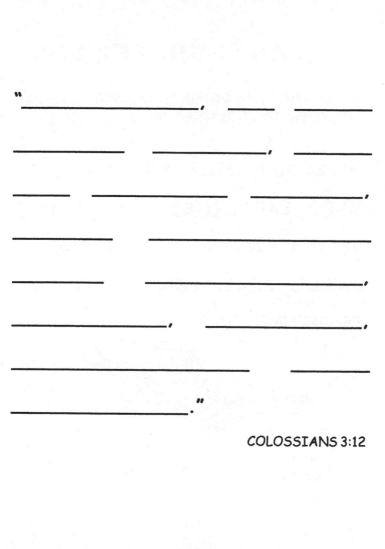

COLOSSIANS 3:12

SCRAMBLED VERSES

UNSCRAMBLE THE WORDS BELOW AND COMPLETE
THE VERSE ON THE NEXT PAGE.

"UTB OUY, NMA FO DGO, LFEE

MRFO LAL ITHS, DAN RPSUUE

GRTHIUEOSSENS, SGOSEDLNI,

AHTIF, VOLE, ECNENDAUR DNA

TSSGEENNEL."

GODLINESS FAITH LOVE ENDURANCE RIGHTEOUSNESS

"_____ _____, _____ _____

_____, _____ _____ _____

_____, _____ _____

_____, _____,

_____, _____, _____

_____ _____."

1 TIMOTHY 6:11

151

SCRAMBLED VERSES

UNSCRAMBLE THE WORDS BELOW AND COMPLETE
THE VERSE ON THE NEXT PAGE.

"UTB NI UYOR RHSTAE EST TPAAR
TCSHIR SA DLRO. SAYLAW EB
PDREERAP OT EGIV NA ARENWS OT
EENVOERY HOW SSKA UYO OT VIGE
EHT SRAENO FRO HET EPHO THTA
YUO VAHE. TUB OD HITS TWHI
SGESENTNEL DNA TRCEEPS."

1 PETER 3:15

THINK, THINK, THINK

GOD IS VERY GENTLE IN HOW HE TEACHES US AND DEALS WITH US. GOD IS NOT PUSHY NOR DOES HE MAKE US DO WHAT HE WANTS US TO DO.

GOD WANTS US TO *FREELY* SEEK HIM AND TO CHOOSE TO DO HIS WILL. GOD WILL NEVER FORCE HIS OWN WAY ON ANYONE. GOD YEARNS TO FILL US WITH HIS LIFE SO THAT WE WILL NOT BE EMPTY ANYMORE.

GOD IS YOUR BEST FRIEND AND HE IS VERY SENSITIVE TO YOUR NEEDS. HE ALWAYS WANTS YOU TO GROW IN YOUR FAITH AND TRUST IN HIM. GOD IS ALWAYS SOFTLY, CALMLY, AND TENDERLY ASKING YOU TO *TRUST* WHAT YOU CANNOT SEE.

GOD IS ALWAYS WILLING TO HELP YOU TO BE GENTLE WITH THOSE AROUND YOU, WANTING YOU TO TREAT OTHERS AS HE TREATS YOU.

AS HE GIVES YOU TRUTH AND ALLOWS YOU TO FREELY MAKE YOUR OWN CHOICES, HE WANTS YOU TO DO THE SAME WITH THE PEOPLE IN YOUR LIFE. GOD WANTS YOU TO BE READY TO SHARE YOUR REASON FOR HOPE WITH *HIS* GENTLENESS AND RESPECT.

HE KNOWS WE NEED HIS HELP TO DO THIS. WHEN YOU ARE TALKING TO OTHERS ABOUT THE LORD, ARE YOU LETTING THE HOLY SPIRIT DO IT THROUGH YOU OR ARE YOU DEPENDING UPON YOURSELF?

WHEN SOMEONE DOES NOT WANT TO LISTEN TO YOU, DO YOU GET ANGRY AND FRUSTRATED? WHAT DO YOU *NEED* TO DO?

SELF-CONTROL

WHAT IS SELF-CONTROL? TO BE SELF-CONTROLLED MEANS TO SHOW RESTRAINT, TO BE SELF-DISCIPLINED, DISCRETE, PATIENT, RESPECTFUL, AND TO BE WILLING TO MAKE THE CHOICE TO DO WHAT IS RIGHT AND GOOD.

THESE ARE ALL NOBLE CHARACTER TRAITS BUT AT MANY TIMES IN OUR LIVES, VERY HARD TO LIVE OUT.

GOD *ALWAYS* SHOWS RESTRAINT IN WHAT HE CHOOSES TO DO AND HOW HE DEALS WITH HIS CHILDREN. AT ANY TIME, GOD HAS THE POWER AND THE AUTHORITY TO HAVE HIS CHILDREN BE AND DO WHAT HE WANTS. YET, GOD DOES NOT WORK LIKE THAT. HE IS VERY RESPECTFUL OF OUR CHOICES AND IS FOREVER PATIENT WITH US.

GOD ALWAYS CHOOSES TO DO WHAT IS RIGHT AND GOOD FOR YOU. GOD DOES NOT PUSH HIS OWN WILL AND DESIRES ON YOU. HE WANTS YOU TO *CHOOSE* HIM, TO FOLLOW HIM, AND TO LOVE HIM BY YOUR OWN DESIRE.

HE GIVES YOU THE FREEDOM TO CHOOSE IN YOUR LIVES AND IS RESPECTFUL OF YOUR CHOICES. HE DOES NOT FORCE HIMSELF OR HIS WILL ON YOU IN ANY WAY.

IF YOU FIND THAT YOU LACK SELF-CONTROL IN YOUR LIFE, WHO SHOULD YOU ASK IF THIS IS SOMETHING YOU REALLY DESIRE TO HAVE?

SCRAMBLED VERSES

UNSCRAMBLE THE WORDS BELOW AND COMPLETE THE VERSE ON THE NEXT PAGE.

"KMEA TI RYUO ANOMBITI OT EDAL A TQUEI FLEI, OT NDIM OYUR WON SBUSSENI DNA OT KWRO HWTI RYUO SHDAN, SJTU AS EW DTLO UYO, OS TTHA RYUO YDLAI ELFI YMA NWI EHT TRECESP FO SORUTESDI DAN OS TAHT UYO LIWL NTO EB TDNEEPEDN NO YABDOYN."

1 THESSALONIANS 4:11–12

UNSCRAMBLE THE WORDS FROM THE LIST BELOW. THEN USE THE CIRCLED LETTERS ON THE NEXT PAGE TO COMPLETE THE VERSE.

1. RFEFTO
2. ITMBIANO
3. ENM
4. TUEIQ
5. ENDEPD
6. ILFE
7. DOTL
8. YBDO

160

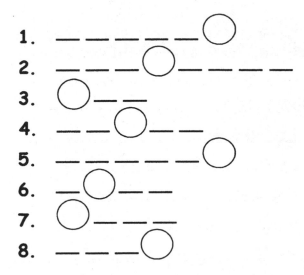

1. _ _ _ _ _ ◯
2. _ _ _ ◯ _ _ _ _
3. ◯ _ _
4. _ _ ◯ _ _
5. _ _ _ _ _ ◯
6. _ ◯ _ _
7. ◯ _ _ _
8. _ _ _ ◯

"FOR GOD DID NOT GIVE US A SPIRIT
OF _ _ _ _ _ _ _ _, BUT A
SPIRIT OF POWER, OF LOVE AND OF
SELF-DISCIPLINE."

2 TIMOTHY 1:7

SCRAMBLED CIRCLES

UNSCRAMBLE THE WORDS FROM THE LIST BELOW. THEN USE THE CIRCLED LETTERS ON THE NEXT PAGE TO COMPLETE THE VERSE.

1. EEJRICO
2. EDORFEM
3. FESL
4. ORDUP
5. NEO
6. ARECET
7. RUAETN

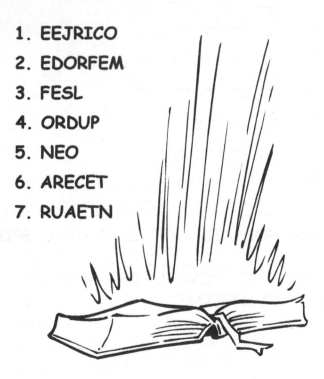

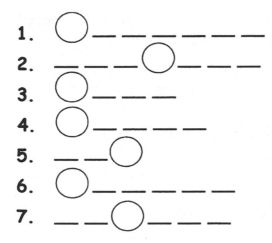

1. ◯ _ _ _ _ _
2. _ _ _ ◯ _ _ _
3. ◯ _ _ _
4. ◯ _ _ _ _
5. _ _ ◯
6. ◯ _ _ _ _ _
7. _ _ ◯ _ _ _

"TEACH THE OLDER MEN TO BE TEMPERATE, WORTHY OF _ _ _ _ _ _ _, SELF-CONTROLLED, AND SOUND IN FAITH, IN LOVE AND IN ENDURANCE."

TITUS 2:2

163

SCRAMBLED VERSES

UNSCRAMBLE THE WORDS BELOW AND COMPLETE THE VERSE ON THE NEXT PAGE.

"TI SI OTN OGDO OT ETA OTO CMHU NYOHE, RNO SI TI EHLONBOAR OT EKSE ESN'O WNO NROHO. KILE A TCIY SHWOE LAWLS REA NBEKRO WDNO SI A NMA HOW CLKSA ELSF-LCOORNT."

"____ ____ ____ ____
____ ____ ____ ____
____, ____ ____ __ ____
_____ __ ____ ____
____ ____ ____.
____ ____ ____
____ ____ ____
____ ____ ____
____ ____ ____ ____
____-____."

PROVERBS 25:27–28

165

THINK, THINK, THINK

GOD WANTS YOU TO LIVE A LIFE OF SELF-CONTROL . WHAT DOES THIS ACTUALLY MEAN?

IT MEANS PUTTING YOURSELF UNDER *GOD'S* CONTROL. DEPENDING UPON HIM AND THE HOLY SPIRIT TO GUIDE YOU AND LIVE THROUGH YOU. THIS IS SOMETHING YOU HAVE TO DO MOMENT BY MOMENT.

GOD WANTS YOU GIVE HIM YOUR THOUGHTS AND LET HIM MAKE THEM THE SAME AS HIS THOUGHTS; HE WANTS TO MAKE YOUR WILL HIS WILL; HE WANTS TO MAKE YOUR WAY OF DOING THINGS HIS WAY OF DOING THINGS.

GOD WANTS YOU TO *UNDERSTAND* HE KNOWS WHAT THE NEXT MOMENT HOLDS AND WHAT IS GOING TO HAPPEN IN TOMORROW. HE WANTS YOU TO THINK OF YOURSELF AS BEING BLIND AND ALLOW HIM TO DIRECT YOU. HE KNOWS BEST THE WAY YOU SHOULD LIVE AND THE CHOICES YOU SHOULD MAKE.

GOD WANTS YOU TO KNOW HIM AS YOUR VERY SOURCE OF LIFE AND LET HIS LIFE LIVE IN YOU AND THROUGH YOU.

THIS WILL HAPPEN ONLY WHEN YOU TOTALLY DEPEND ON HIM FOR *EVERYTHING*.

DEPENDING ON THE HOLY SPIRIT IS WHAT JESUS MEANT WHEN HE SAID THAT HE WAS THE VINE AND WE ARE THE BRANCHES—THAT IF WE DEPEND ON HIM, WE WOULD BEAR MUCH FRUIT.

THE FRUIT YOU WILL BEAR IS GOD'S FRUIT. YOU CAN NOT BEAR GOD'S FRUIT BY YOUR OWN POWER AND THAT IS WHY GOD GAVE YOU HIS HOLY SPIRIT. HIS HOLY SPIRIT WILL BEAR GOD'S FRUIT *IN YOU AND IN YOUR LIFE.*

ARE *YOU* TRYING TO PRODUCE GOD'S FRUIT OR ARE YOU DEPENDING UPON GOD?

WRAP IT UP!

IN THIS BOOK YOU HAVE LEARNED WHAT THE FRUIT OF THE SPIRIT IS AND HOW THE FRUIT LIVES *THROUGH* THE HOLY SPIRIT.

TRYING TO BE ALL THESE THINGS YOURSELF IS IMPOSSIBLE. WE MAY AT TIMES BE *SOME* OF THESE THINGS, BUT WE CANNOT BE ALL OF THESE THINGS ALL OF THE TIME.

ONLY GOD CAN BE ALL THESE THINGS ALL OF THE TIME. GOD WANTS US TO KNOW THE FRUIT OF THE SPIRIT, NOT SO WE SHOULD TRY AND LIVE IT BY OUR OWN EFFORT OR POWER, BUT SO WE WOULD KNOW WHO HE IS AND LET HIM LIVE THROUGH US.

GOD IS PATIENT, GOD IS KIND.

GOD DOES NOT ENVY, GOD DOES NOT BOAST,
GOD IS NOT PROUD.

GOD IS NOT RUDE. GOD IS NOT SELF- SEEKING,
GOD IS NOT EASILY ANGERED, GOD KEEPS
NO RECORD OF WRONGS.

GOD DOES NOT DELIGHT IN EVIL BUT REJOICES
WITH THE TRUTH.

GOD ALWAYS PROTECTS, GOD ALWAYS
TRUSTS, GOD ALWAYS HOPES, GOD ALWAYS
PERSEVERES.

GOD NEVER FAILS.

Super Silly STORIES

INSTRUCTIONS

Everyone likes a good story—especially one that makes you laugh till you're out of breath! And that's what *Super Silly Stories* is all about.

These stories *seem* normal enough, with titles like "A Letter from Camp" or "My Birthday." But each one has several blanks for *you* to fill in—and the words you pick may make it the silliest story ever!

First, you'll need to know some "school things" like what a noun is, or an adjective, or other parts of speech. Don't let that scare you! If you need some help on those, check out the "Definitions and Examples" on page 174.

Once you have your parts of speech under control, turn to the first "Word List" page—but don't look ahead. Fill in the blanks, (either by yourself, or better yet, with friends) and *then* turn to the story. Put the words you chose into the right blanks in the story, and see what happens. It'll be silly for sure!

To make some *really* silly stories, pick really good words! If the story asks for an adjective, rather than just saying "big," say "humongous." If it asks for a noun, pick something strange like "meteorite" or "platypus." The more unusual, the better.

Are you ready for a good laugh? Then get to it—*Super Silly Stories* awaits you!

PARTS OF SPEECH—
DEFINITIONS AND EXAMPLES

Noun: A person, place, or thing (teacher, factory, lamp)

Plural noun: More than one person, place, or thing (teachers, factories, lamps)

Verb: An action word (walk, beg, love)

Verb "-ing": An action word that end with -ing (walking, begging, loving)

Verb "-ed": An action word that ends with -ed (walked, begged, loved)

Adjective: A word that describes a noun (happy, enormous, green)

Place: Any place (Texas, France, Africa)

Liquid: Any liquid (oil, soup, shampoo)

Number: Any number (1; 518; 4, 875, 926)

Funny word: Any funny-sounding word, real, or made-up (bloof, plop, zing)

Exclamation: Any word spoken excitedly (hooray, wow, kazaam)

Name of son: Any song ("If You're Happy and You Know It," "Old McDonald," "This Little Light of Mine")

Name of person: Any person (Natalie, Mrs. Jones, Michael Jordan)

175

WORD LIST

(adjective) _____

(number) _____

(adjective) _____

(adjective) _____

(adjective) _____

(adjective) _____

(noun) _____

(number) _____

(verb) _____

(verb) _____

(number) _____

(verb) _____

(adjective) _____

A LETTER FROM CAMP

Dear Mom and Dad,

I'm having a _____ time at camp!
(ADJECTIVE)

My _____ roommates are a lot of fun!
(NUMBER)

At night, we tell _____ stories and
(ADJECTIVE)

_____ jokes before going to sleep.
(ADJECTIVE)

The food is _____. For breakfast,
(ADJECTIVE)

we had _____ eggs and
(ADJECTIVE)

_____. I ate _____
(NOUN)   (NUMBER)

servings!

During free time, I like to _____.
(VERB)

I am also learning how to _____!
(VERB)

I miss you, but I'll be home in _____
(NUMBER)

days. I promise I'll _____
(VERB)

again soon.

Love,
Your _____ child
(ADJECTIVE)

WORD LIST

(adjective) _____

(adjective) _____

(verb) _____

(adjective) _____

(noun) _____

(verb) _____

(plural noun) _____

(verb) _____

(plural noun) _____

(adjective) _____

(verb) _____

MIND YOUR MANNERS

Always keep a _____ attitude.
(ADJECTIVE)

Be _____ to others.
(ADJECTIVE)

Never _____ with your mouth full.
(VERB)

When indoors, use _____
(ADJECTIVE)
voices.

Use a _____ to _____
(NOUN)   (VERB)
your face during mealtime.

Keep your _____ to yourself.
(PLURAL NOUN)

Don't _____ when others are
(VERB)

talking.

Share your _____ with
(PLURAL NOUN)

others.

Always use _____ words.
(ADJECTIVE)

When someone does something kind,

_____ them.
(VERB)

WORD LIST

(adjective) _____

(adjective) _____

(number) _____

(number) _____

(adjective) _____

(verb) _____

(plural noun) _____

(verb) _____

(noun) _____

(noun) _____

(noun) _____

(funny word) _____

(exclamation) _____

(adjective) _____

(adjective) _____

A VISIT TO THE DOCTOR

Today I went to the doctor's. I felt a

little _____, and knew I'd feel
    (ADJECTIVE)

_____ when it was over.
  (ADJECTIVE)

The nurse told me I weigh _____
                                     (NUMBER)

pounds and am _____ inches tall.
            (NUMBER)

She was very _____.
      (ADJECTIVE)

Then, I saw the doctor _____
                        (VERB)

through the door. He asked me a few

_____, and began to
(PLURAL NOUN)

_____ me.
  (VERB)

185

He listed to my _____ and
(NOUN)

checked my _____. Then he
(NOUN)

told me to open my _____ and
(NOUN)

say _____. "_____,"
(FUNNY WORD)   (EXCLAMATION)

he said. "Everything looks _____.
(ADJECTIVE)

You are a very _____ youngster!"
(ADJECTIVE)

186

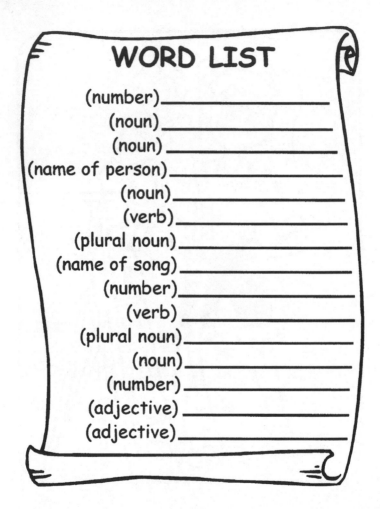

WORD LIST

(number)_____

(noun)_____

(noun)_____

(name of person)_____

(noun)_____

(verb)_____

(plural noun)_____

(name of song)_____

(number)_____

(verb)_____

(plural noun)_____

(noun)_____

(number)_____

(adjective)_____

(adjective)_____

MY BIRTHDAY

On my birthday, _____ guests
(NUMBER)
were invited to my party. When they

arrived, we played Pin the _____
(NOUN)
on the _____. _____
(NOUN)   (NAME OF PERSON)
was closest, pinning it on the

_____.
(NOUN)
Next, I got to _____ out the
(VERB)
_____ on my cake while every
(PLURAL NOUN)
one sang _____. I extinguished
(NAME OF SONG)
all _____ of them!
(NUMBER)

After we ate, I got to _____
(VERB)
my _____. My favorite one was
(PLURAL NOUN)
the cool _____. I've wanted
(NOUN)
one for _____ years!
(NUMBER)
When the party was over, we were all

_____ and everyone went home.
(ADJECTIVE)
It had been a _____ day.
(ADJECTIVE)

WORD LIST

(place)_____

(name of person)_____

(adjective)_____

(verb)_____

(verb)_____

(noun)_____

(number)_____

(verb)_____

(plural noun)_____

(plural noun)_____

(plural noun)_____

(adjective)_____

MY DREAM VACATION

If I could go anywhere on vacation, I'd

go to _____. I would take
        (PLACE)

_____ and we would fly on a
(NAME OF PERSON)

_____ airplane.
    (ADJECTIVE)

While we were there, we would

_____ different kinds of food
     (VERB)

and _____ many different
          (VERB)

places. We'd also be sure to swim in the

_____.
    (NOUN)

We would spend _____ days
(NUMBER)

there, then _____ back home
(VERB)

with many _____ and
(PLURAL NOUN)

_____. There would be many
(PLURAL NOUN)

stories to tell our _____, and
(PLURAL NOUN)

we would remember our trip for a

_____ time.
(ADJECTIVE)

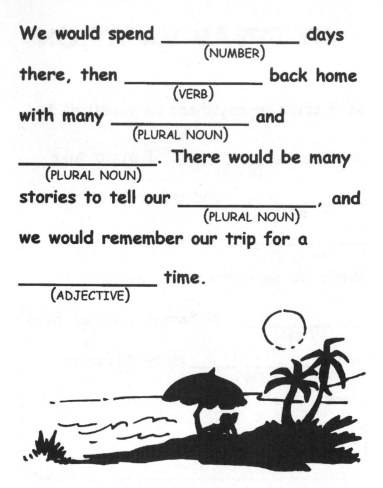

WORD LIST

(verb)_____

(noun)_____

(noun) _____

(noun) _____

(verb)_____

(verb) _____

(noun)_____

(noun) _____

(adjective) _____

(verb)_____

(verb)_____

(adjective) _____

(plural noun) _____

SAFETY WARNINGS

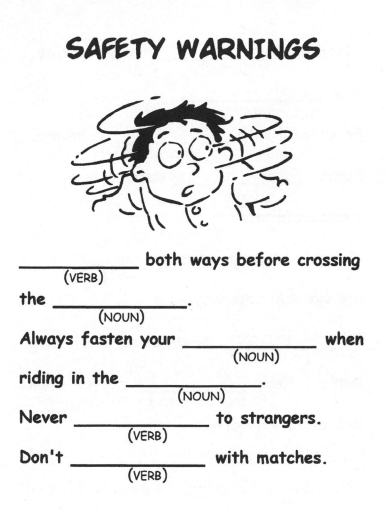

_____ both ways before crossing
(VERB)

the _____.
(NOUN)

Always fasten your _____ when
(NOUN)

riding in the _____.
(NOUN)

Never _____ to strangers.
(VERB)

Don't _____ with matches.
(VERB)

Wear a _____ when you ride (NOUN)

your _____. (NOUN)

Be careful with _____ knives. (ADJECTIVE)

Never _____ outside in a (VERB)

thunderstorm.

To avoid slipping, always _____ (VERB)

around the swimming pool.

Be _____ when using electricity. (ADJECTIVE)

Replace the _____ in your smoke (PLURAL NOUN)

detectors regularly.

WORD LIST

(noun) _____

(verb) _____

(noun) _____

(liquid) _____

(noun) _____

(verb "-ing") _____

JACK AND JILL

Jack and Jill went up the _____
(NOUN)

To _____ a _____ of
(VERB)   (NOUN)

_____.
(LIQUID)

Jack fell down

And broke his _____,
(NOUN)

And Jill came _____ after.
(VERB "-ING")

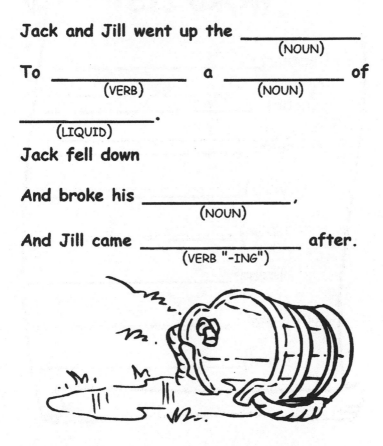

WORD LIST

(adjective)_____

(noun) _____

(plural noun) _____

(verb) _____

(noun)_____

(noun)_____

(verb "-ed")_____

(place)_____

THE OLD WOMAN WHO LIVED IN A SHOE

There was an _____ woman
(ADJECTIVE)

Who lived in a _____.
(NOUN)

She had so many _____,
(PLURAL NOUN)

She didn't know what to _____.
(VERB)

She gave them some _____,
(NOUN)

Without any _____,
(NOUN)

And _____ them all soundly
(VERB "-ED")

And sent them to _____.
(PLACE)

WORD LIST

(noun) _____

(noun) _____

(plural noun) _____

(verb) _____

(plural noun) _____

(verb) _____

GEORGIE PORGIE

Georgie Porgie, _____ and
                      (NOUN)

_____,
  (NOUN)

Kissed the _____ and made
             (PLURAL NOUN)

them _____.
      (VERB)

When the _____ came out to
          (PLURAL NOUN)

_____,
  (VERB)

Georgie Porgie ran away.

WORD LIST

(noun)_____

(plural noun)_____

(noun)_____

(adjective)_____

(name of person)_____

(noun)_____

(liquid)_____

(noun)_____

(adjective)_____

(adjective)_____

(adjective)_____

(verb)_____

THE AMUSEMENT PARK

I love going to the amusement park. I

like to ride the __RoLLercoster__ It goes
                        (NOUN)

so fast, and I put my ___arm's___
                    (PLURAL NOUN)

high over my ___head___.
                (NOUN)

Then, it's on to the __Bumper__
                        (ADJECTIVE)

cars. It's fun to bump __My Firehds__
                        (NAME OF PERSON)

_____.
    (NOUN)

When it's hot outside, my favorite ride

is the _____ slide. I get
(LIQUID)

splashed in the _____, and I
(NOUN)

get off looking quite _____.
(ADJECTIVE)

The rides are _____, and by
(ADJECTIVE)

the end of the day, I feel

_____. But I always look
(ADJECTIVE)

forward to when I can _____
(VERB)

again!

WORD LIST

(adjective) _____

(noun) _____

(noun) _____

(verb) _____

(adjective) _____

(number) _____

(noun) _____

(liquid) _____

(adjective) _____

(number) _____

(exclamation) _____

(adjective) _____

(verb) _____

(adjective) _____

(adjective) _____

TOOTHPASTE COMMERCIAL

Do you find your teeth looking

_____? Then do we have a
   (ADJECTIVE)

_____ for you! All you need to
   (NOUN)

do is put some on a _____,
                    (NOUN)

and _____ your teeth. For
    (VERB)

_____ results, use it
   (ADJECTIVE)

_____ times each day, and
   (NUMBER)

rinse your _____ with
           (NOUN)

_____ when you're finished.
   (LIQUID)

213

We guarantee that your teeth will be looking _____ in just
(ADJECTIVE)
_____ days. And on your next
(NUMBER)
trip to the dentist, he will be sure to

say, "_____! You have been
(EXCLAMATION)
taking very _____ care of your
(ADJECTIVE)
teeth!"

We know that you'll _____ this
(VERB)
toothpaste. Remember, a _____
(ADJECTIVE)
mouth is a _____ mouth.
(ADJECTIVE)

WORD LIST

(adjective) _____

(plural noun) _____

(liquid) _____

(verb) _____

(noun) _____

(adjective) _____

(noun) _____

(noun) _____

(adjective) _____

(number) _____

(adjective) _____

(verb) _____

(noun) _____

(verb) _____

(adjective) _____

THE WEATHER FORECAST

Today will be _____ with a
(ADJECTIVE)

chance of _____. We might even
(PLURAL NOUN)

have a few _____ showers. If
(LIQUID)

you go out, be sure to _____
(VERB)

your _____!
(NOUN)

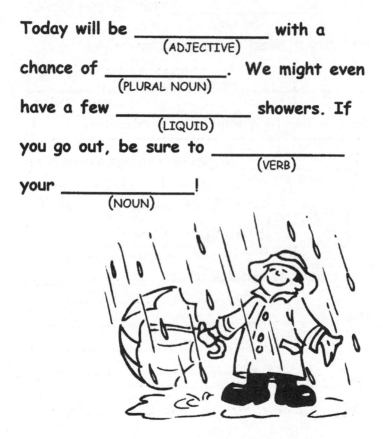

Tomorrow will be very _____,
(ADJECTIVE)
and the _____ will be shining.
(NOUN)
You might need to wear your

_____. It will be a _____
(NOUN)   (ADJECTIVE)
day, with the temperature reaching

_____ degrees. It would be a
(NUMBER)
_____ day to _____ in
(ADJECTIVE)   (VERB)
the park or ride your _____. If
(NOUN)
you can, get outside and _____
(VERB)
the _____ air.
(ADJECTIVE)

WORD LIST

(adjective) _____

(verb) _____

(verb) _____

(adjective) _____

(noun) _____

(verb) _____

(noun) _____

(adjective) _____

(noun) _____

(verb) _____

(plural noun) _____

(adjective) _____

(plural noun) _____

(noun) _____

(adjective) _____

(plural noun) _____

(liquid) _____

(adjective) _____

A DAY AT THE BEACH

When going to the beach, you'll want to

wear your _____ suit so you're
         (ADJECTIVE)

ready to _____. It's important
        (VERB)

to _____ on plenty of
   (VERB)

_____ lotion so you don't get a
(ADJECTIVE)

_____.
(NOUN)

You'll want to _____ sunglasses
        (VERB)

to keep the _____ out of your
      (NOUN)

eyes. It's also a _____ idea to
       (ADJECTIVE)

take along a _____ to dry
     (NOUN)

yourself off after you _____.
          (VERB)

To protect your _____ from the
(PLURAL NOUN)
_____ sand, you may want to
(ADJECTIVE)
wear _____.
(PLURAL NOUN)
Don't forget to take a _____
(NOUN)
to float on, a _____ ball, and
(ADJECTIVE)
some fun _____ to play in the
(PLURAL NOUN)
sand. Drink plenty of _____,
(LIQUID)
and above all, have a _____
(ADJECTIVE)
day.

WORD LIST

(noun)_____

(adjective)_____

(plural noun)_____

(noun)_____

(adjective)_____

(noun)_____

(noun)_____

(noun)_____

(adjective)_____

(verb)_____

(noun)_____

(plural noun)_____

(name of song)_____

(noun)_____

(adjective)_____

LET'S GO CAMPING!

My family likes to go camping. When we

arrive at the camping spot, we pitch

the _____. This can be a

(NOUN)

_____ job. We then put our

(ADJECTIVE)

sleeping _____ inside.

(PLURAL NOUN)

It's my sister's job to get wood for the

_____. When it gets _____,
(NOUN)   (ADJECTIVE)

my mom cooks _____ over it.
                   (NOUN)

Usually we eat _____ and
                   (NOUN)

_____. It always tastes
(NOUN)

_____.
(ADJECTIVE)

When it's dark, we _____ around
                        (VERB)

the fire and look up at the _____
                                  (NOUN)

and _____ in the sky. Sometimes
      (PLURAL NOUN)

we sing _____. Then, it's time
            (NAME OF SONG)

for _____.
        (NOUN)

We always have a _____ time
                        (ADJECTIVE)

camping together as a family!

WORD LIST

(adjective) _____

(verb) _____

(adjective) _____

(adjective) _____

(verb) _____

(noun) _____

(noun) _____

(verb) _____

(noun) _____

(plural noun) _____

(noun) _____

(number) _____

(noun) _____

(verb) _____

(adjective) _____

(adjective) _____

RECESS

When it's time for recess, my class gets

in a _____ line, and we
      (ADJECTIVE)

_____ down the hall and go
   (VERB)

outside to the _____ playground.
         (ADJECTIVE)

We like going outside, because we can

use _____ voices, and
   (ADJECTIVE)

_____.
  (VERB)

Usually, the boys play _____
          (NOUN)

or _____ and the girls
  (NOUN)

_____ or play _____.
  (VERB)   (NOUN)

Everyone takes turns swinging on the

_____ or climbing on the
(PLURAL NOUN)

_____.
(NOUN)

After _____ minutes, the
(NUMBER)

teacher blows the _____. We
(NOUN)

_____ and get in a
(VERB)

_____ line to go back inside,
(ADJECTIVE)

looking forward to the next

_____ recess.
(ADJECTIVE)

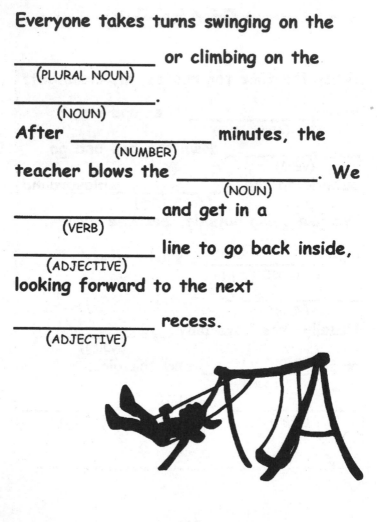

WORD LIST

(noun) _____

(noun) _____

(adjective) _____

(plural noun) _____

(noun) _____

(plural noun) _____

(adjective) _____

(plural noun) _____

(adjective) _____

(noun) _____

(adjective) _____

(adjective) _____

(adjective) _____

(adjective) _____

(noun) _____

(noun) _____

(noun) _____

ON THE MENU

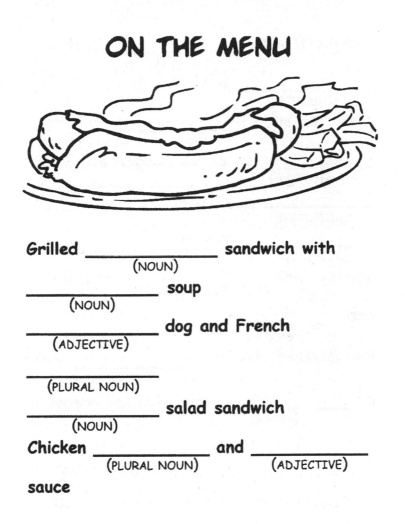

Grilled _____ sandwich with
(NOUN)

_____ soup
(NOUN)

_____ dog and French
(ADJECTIVE)

_____
(PLURAL NOUN)

_____ salad sandwich
(NOUN)

Chicken _____ and _____
(PLURAL NOUN)   (ADJECTIVE)

sauce

Spaghetti with _____ and
              (PLURAL NOUN)

_____ bread
(ADJECTIVE)

Macaroni and _____
              (NOUN)

_____ cheeseburger with
(ADJECTIVE)

_____ chips
(ADJECTIVE)

_____ ravioli
(ADJECTIVE)

Turkey with _____ potatoes
          (ADJECTIVE)

and _____
    (NOUN)

For dessert, try the _____ cake
            (NOUN)

or _____ pie with ice cream.
  (NOUN)

WORD LIST

(verb) _____

(verb) _____

(verb) _____

(noun) _____

(noun) _____

(plural noun) _____

(adjective) _____

(noun) _____

(noun) _____

(noun) _____

(verb) _____

(verb) _____

(adjective) _____

(noun) _____

RULES OF THE ROAD

Always _____ at a _____
(VERB)   (VERB)

sign.

Be sure to _____ the
(VERB)

_____ limit.
(NOUN)

Use your _____ signal when
(NOUN)

making a turn.

When it's dark, drive with your

_____ on.
(PLURAL NOUN)

Keep a _____ distance between
(ADJECTIVE)

your _____ and the one in
(NOUN)

front of you.

Turn on the _____
(NOUN)
wipers when driving in the _____.
(NOUN)
When a traffic light is green, _____.
(VERB)
When it's red, _____. When
(VERB)
the light is _____, slow down.
(ADJECTIVE)
Always wear your _____ belt.
(NOUN)

WORD LIST

(noun) _____

(noun) _____

(noun) _____

(verb "-ed") _____

(noun) _____

(adjective) _____

(noun) _____

(verb "-ed") _____

(noun) _____

(noun) _____

HEY DIDDLE, DIDDLE

Hey diddle, diddle,

The _____ and the _____,
        (NOUN)   (NOUN)

The _____ _____
        (NOUN)   (VERB "-ED")

over the _____;
          (NOUN)

The _____ _____
       (ADJECTIVE)   (NOUN)

_____
(VERB "-ED")

To see such sport,

And the _____ ran away with
         (NOUN)

the _____.
     (NOUN)

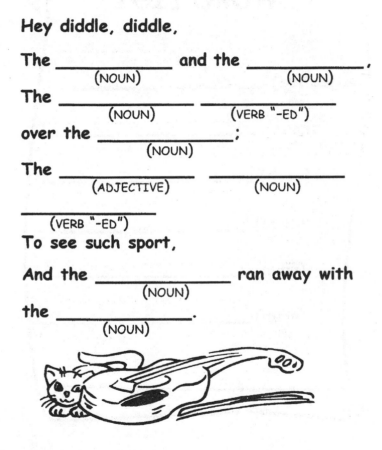

WORD LIST

(adjective) _____

(noun) _____

(verb) _____

(noun) _____

(noun) _____

(noun) _____

TWINKLE, TWINKLE, LITTLE STAR

Twinkle, twinkle, _____
(ADJECTIVE)

_____,
(NOUN)

How I _____ what you are!
(VERB)

Up above the _____ so high,
(NOUN)

Like a _____ in the
(NOUN)

_____.
(NOUN)

WORD LIST

(verb) _____

(verb) _____

(verb) _____

(verb) _____

(adjective) _____

(noun) _____

(noun) _____

(verb) _____

(noun) _____

(verb) _____

(adjective) _____

(plural noun) _____

(verb) _____

THINGS I DO TO HELP AROUND THE HOUSE

_____ my room and _____
   (VERB)   (VERB)
my bed.

Help _____ dinner.
        (VERB)

_____ the _____ dishes
  (VERB)   (ADJECTIVE)
and put them in the _____.
                     (NOUN)

Take out the _____.
(NOUN)

_____ the car.
(VERB)

Take the _____ for a walk.
(NOUN)

_____ the _____
(VERB)   (ADJECTIVE)

laundry.

Vacuum the _____.
(PLURAL NOUN)

_____ the furniture.
(VERB)

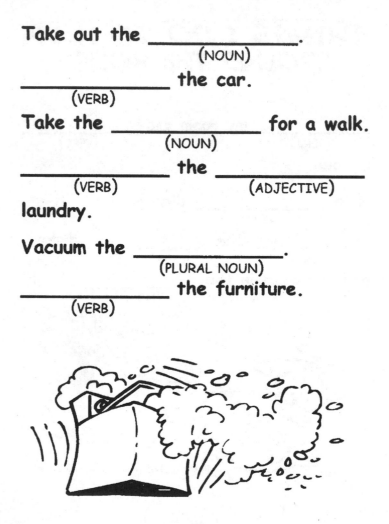

WORD LIST

(adjective) _____

(verb "-ed") _____

(noun) _____

(verb "-ing") _____

(plural noun) _____

(noun) _____

(noun) _____

(verb "-ed") _____

LITTLE MISS MUFFET

_____ Miss Muffet
(ADJECTIVE)

_____ on a _____,
(VERB "-ED")   (NOUN)

_____ her _____ and
(VERB "-ING")   (PLURAL NOUN)

_____;
(NOUN)

Along came a _____,
(NOUN)

Who sat down beside her,

And _____ Miss Muffet away.
(VERB "-ED")

WORD LIST

(noun) _____

(noun) _____

(noun) _____

(number) _____

(noun) _____

HICKORY, DICKORY, DOCK

Hickory, dickory, dock,

The _____ ran up the
       (NOUN)

_____.
   (NOUN)

The _____ struck _____,
      (NOUN)   (NUMBER)

The _____ ran down,
      (NOUN)

Hickory, dickory, dock.

WORD LIST

(noun) _____

(adjective) _____

(noun) _____

(verb) _____

(adjective) _____

(adjective) _____

(verb) _____

(adjective) _____

(funny word) _____

(noun) _____

(verb) _____

(noun) _____

(adjective) _____

IF I WERE A SUPERHERO...

If I were a superhero, my name would be

Super _____ . I would wear a
      (NOUN)

_____ _____ , and
   (ADJECTIVE)   (NOUN)

would _____ really fast! I'd have
          (VERB)

_____ vision, and _____
   (ADJECTIVE)   (ADJECTIVE)

muscles so that I could _____
                              (VERB)

_____ things if I needed to.
   (ADJECTIVE)

When people saw me they'd shout,

"_____ ! Our _____ is
   (FUNNY WORD)   (NOUN)

here!"

"Yes," I'd answer. "I want to

_____ people, and make the
(VERB)

_____ a _____ place
(NOUN)   (ADJECTIVE)

to live!"

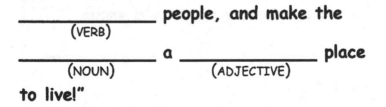

WORD LIST

(name of person) _____

(adjective) _____

(name of place) _____

(adjective) _____

(adjective) _____

(noun) _____

(plural noun) _____

(noun) _____

(number) _____

(plural noun) _____

(plural noun) _____

(adjective) _____

(verb) _____

(adjective) _____

(noun) _____

A VACATION POSTCARD

Dear _____,
(NAME OF PERSON)

I'm having a _____ vacation!
(ADJECTIVE)

_____ is a _____ place,
(NAME OF PLACE)   (ADJECTIVE)

and we have had _____ weather.
(ADJECTIVE)

The _____ has been shining every
(NOUN)

day!

I've bought some _____ on our
(PLURAL NOUN)

trip, and even got a cool _____
(NOUN)

for you. I've taken at least _____
(NUMBER)

pictures of interesting _____ and
(PLURAL NOUN)

_____.
(PLURAL NOUN)

I have tried some _____ food,
(ADJECTIVE)

too. I'll tell you all about it when I

_____ you.
(VERB)

Have a _____ day!
(ADJECTIVE)

Your _____ always.
(NOUN)

WORD LIST

(verb) _____

(noun) _____

(number) _____

(verb) _____

(adjective) _____

(noun) _____

(noun) _____

(plural noun) _____

(verb) _____

(noun) _____

(number) _____

(number) _____

(verb) _____

(adjective) _____

(verb) _____

HOW TO MAKE A PIZZA

To make a pizza, you first need to

_____ the dough in a _____.
      (VERB)   (NOUN)

Next, spread _____ cups of sauce
                     (NUMBER)

on top. After that, _____
                              (VERB)

_____ sauce over the pizza.
   (ADJECTIVE)

Finally, add your favorite toppings, like

_____, _____, and
     (NOUN)   (NOUN)

_____.
  (PLURAL NOUN)

When you've put everything on that you'd like, _____ it in the

(VERB)

_____ at _____ degrees

(NOUN)   (NUMBER)

for _____ minutes. Allow it to

(NUMBER)

cool for a few minutes, then

_____ your _____ pizza.

(VERB)   (ADJECTIVE)

Your family will _____ you!

(VERB)

WORD LIST

(adjective) _____

(number) _____

(number) _____

(adjective) _____

(adjective) _____

(number) _____

(number) _____

(noun) _____

(noun) _____

(noun) _____

(noun) _____

(adjective) _____

(noun) _____

OUR NEW HOUSE

My family just moved into our new house.

It is very _____, with
                (ADJECTIVE)

_____ bedrooms, _____
   (NUMBER)   (NUMBER)

bathrooms, and a _____
               (ADJECTIVE)

kitchen. My bedroom is _____
               (ADJECTIVE)

with _____ windows and
   (NUMBER)

_____ doors. I'm glad I don't
 (NUMBER)

have to share one with my _____
               (NOUN)

anymore!

There is lots of _____ in the backyard,
(NOUN)

backyard, and a _____ where I can ride
(NOUN)

my _____ .
(NOUN)

I'm sure I'll make _____ friends here,
(ADJECTIVE)

and hope they like to play _____ as
(NOUN)

much as I do!

WORD LIST

(noun) _____

(adjective) _____

(adjective) _____

(noun) _____

(adjective) _____

(noun) _____

(noun) _____

(verb) _____

(verb) _____

(plural noun) _____

(noun) _____

(noun) _____

(adjective) _____

(noun) _____

THANKSGIVING

On Thanksgiving, my relatives come to our

_____ for a _____
(NOUN)   (ADJECTIVE)

dinner. Mom makes a _____
(ADJECTIVE)

meal. We have _____ with
(NOUN)

stuffing, _____ potatoes with
(ADJECTIVE)

_____, cranberry _____,
(NOUN)   (NOUN)

and lots more! We all _____ and
(VERB)

_____ during dinner.
(VERB)

When everyone's finished, usually the

women wash the _____, and the
(PLURAL NOUN)

men watch _____ on television.
(NOUN)

We kids usually play _____
(NOUN)

outside.

Thanksgiving is always _____.
(ADJECTIVE)

I'm so thankful for my _____.
(NOUN)

WORD LIST

(adjective) _____

(adjective) _____

(noun) _____

(noun) _____

(verb) _____

(verb) _____

(verb) _____

I'M A LITTLE TEAPOT

I'm a little teapot,

_____ and _____;
(ADJECTIVE)   (ADJECTIVE)

Here is my _____,
(NOUN)

Here is my _____.
(NOUN)

When I get all steamed up,

Hear me _____,
(VERB)

"_____ me over and _____
(VERB)   (VERB)

me out!"

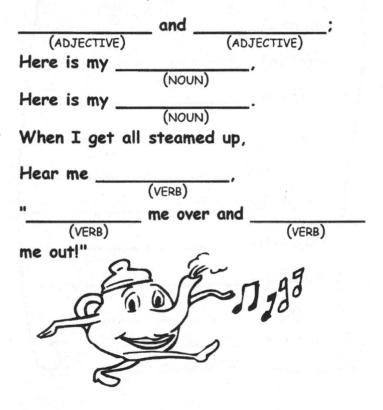

273

WORD LIST

(adjective) _____

(adjective) _____

(noun) _____

(noun) _____

(noun) _____

(noun) _____

(noun) _____

(adjective) _____

(adjective) _____

(noun) _____

THE ITSY BITSY SPIDER

The _____ _____
  (ADJECTIVE)   (ADJECTIVE)
spider climbed up the _____,
                          (NOUN)
Down came the _____ and
                  (NOUN)
washed the _____ out;
              (NOUN)
Out came the _____ and dried
                 (NOUN)
up all the _____,
              (NOUN)
And the _____ _____
          (ADJECTIVE)   (ADJECTIVE)
spider climbed up the _____
                          (NOUN)
again.

WORD LIST

(noun)_____

(noun)_____

(verb)_____

(verb)_____

(noun)_____

(name of person)_____

PAT-A-CAKE, PAT-A-CAKE

Pat-a-cake, pat-a-cake,

Baker's _____,
(NOUN)

Bake me a _____
(NOUN)

As fast as you can!

_____ it and _____ it
(VERB)   (VERB)

And mark it with 'B',

And put it in the _____
(NOUN)

For _____ and me.
(NAME OF PERSON)

WORD LIST

(adjective) _____

(verb) _____

(plural noun) _____

(verb) _____

(adjective) _____

(verb) _____

(adjective) _____

(noun) _____

(verb) _____

(noun) _____

(adjective) _____

(noun) _____

(adjective) _____

(adjective) _____

WINTER FUN

When it snows, there are lots of

_____ things to do outside.
(ADJECTIVE)

It's fun to _____ down the
(VERB)

biggest hill we can find on our

_____. Sometimes we even
(PLURAL NOUN)

_____ each other.
(VERB)

I also like to go _____ skating
(ADJECTIVE)

at the rink. I usually _____ a
(VERB)

lot, but I always have a _____
(ADJECTIVE)

time.

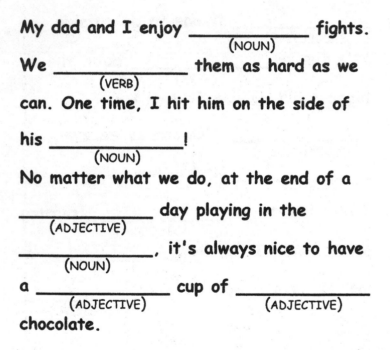

My dad and I enjoy _____ fights.
                     (NOUN)
We _____ them as hard as we
      (VERB)
can. One time, I hit him on the side of

his _____!
      (NOUN)
No matter what we do, at the end of a

_____ day playing in the
   (ADJECTIVE)
_____, it's always nice to have
      (NOUN)
a _____ cup of _____
      (ADJECTIVE)   (ADJECTIVE)
chocolate.

WORD LIST

(adjective) _____

(noun) _____

(verb) _____

(noun) _____

(name of person) _____

(number) _____

(plural noun) _____

(plural noun) _____

(noun) _____

(adjective) _____

(adjective) _____

(adjective) _____

(adjective) _____

(adjective) _____

MY HOBBIES

I have several hobbies that I enjoy. On

_____ days, I like to fly my
(ADJECTIVE)

_____. I get it flying high and
(NOUN)

watch it _____ through the
(VERB)

sky.

I also like to ride my _____.
(NOUN)

Sometimes _____ and I ride
(NAME OF PERSON)

together. The farthest distance we've

traveled is _____ miles. We're
(NUMBER)

always sure to wear our _____
(PLURAL NOUN)

to protect our _____.
(PLURAL NOUN)

I have a _____ collection, too.
(NOUN)

It's always fun to find _____
(ADJECTIVE)

items to add to my collection.

It's important to have _____
(ADJECTIVE)

hobbies. They can make you feel

_____ after a _____
(ADJECTIVE)   (ADJECTIVE)

day, or just be a _____ way to
(ADJECTIVE)

spend your free time.

WORD LIST

(noun) _____

(adjective) _____

(adjective) _____

(verb) _____

(number) _____

(name of song) _____

(adjective) _____

(adjective) _____

(adjective) _____

(number) _____

(verb) _____

(adjective) _____

(adjective) _____

MUSIC LESSONS

I am learning how to play the

_____. It is a _____
(NOUN)   (ADJECTIVE)

instrument, and very _____ to
                        (ADJECTIVE)

learn. Each day, I _____
                      (VERB)

_____ minutes. For my recital,
(NUMBER)

I will play _____. My sister
              (NAME OF SONG)

says it sounds _____, but I
                  (ADJECTIVE)

think it sounds _____.
                  (ADJECTIVE)

My music teacher is very _____.
(ADJECTIVE)

She gives me _____ new songs
(NUMBER)

to learn each week and reminds me to

_____ a lot. She says that if I
(VERB)

keep practicing, I will become a

_____ musician. Just think how
(ADJECTIVE)

_____ that will be!
(ADJECTIVE)

WORD LIST

(adjective) _____

(name of place) _____

(adjective) _____

(name of place) _____

(adjective) _____

(noun) _____

(adjective) _____

(adjective) _____

(exclamation) _____

THIS LITTLE PIGGY

This _____ piggy went to
          (ADJECTIVE)

_____,
(NAME OF PLACE)

This _____ piggy stayed at
          (ADJECTIVE)

_____,
(NAME OF PLACE)

This _____ piggy had roast
          (ADJECTIVE)

_____,
(NOUN)

This _____ piggy had none,
          (ADJECTIVE)

And this _____ piggy cried
          (ADJECTIVE)

_____
(EXCLAMATION)

All the way home.

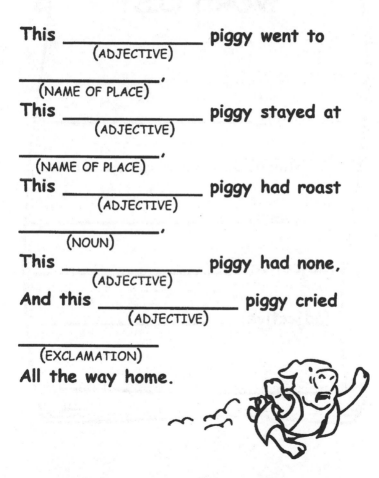

291

WORD LIST

(noun) _____

(noun) _____

(verb) _____

(adjective) _____

(adjective) _____

PETER, PETER, PUMPKIN EATER

Peter, Peter, _____ eater,
                    (NOUN)

Had a _____ and couldn't
          (NOUN)

_____ her,
   (VERB)

He put her in a _____ shell,
                      (ADJECTIVE)

And there he kept her very _____.
                                  (ADJECTIVE)

WORD LIST

(verb) _____

(verb) _____

(plural noun) _____

(verb) _____

(liquid) _____

(verb) _____

(noun) _____

(plural noun) _____

(noun) _____

(plural noun) _____

(verb) _____

(verb) _____

(plural noun) _____

(adjective) _____

(adjective) _____

(adjective) _____

(adjective) _____

IN THE GARDEN

Each year, we _____ a garden.
(VERB)

When the soil is ready, we _____
(VERB)

the _____ in the dirt and
(PLURAL NOUN)

_____ them. Next, we sprinkle
(VERB)

them with _____.
(LIQUID)

The seeds soon _____, reaching
(VERB)

up toward the _____.
(NOUN)

The small, green _____ need
(PLURAL NOUN)

sunshine and _____ to
(NOUN)

grow. _____ begin to grow
(PLURAL NOUN)

around the plants, so we have to

_____ them.
(VERB)

Finally, it's time to _____ the
(VERB)

ripe _____. We have _____
(PLURAL NOUN) (ADJECTIVE)

carrots, _____ tomatoes, and
(ADJECTIVE)

many other _____ vegetables.
(ADJECTIVE)

Food from the garden always tastes

_____!
(ADJECTIVE)

WORD LIST

(verb) _____

(adjective) _____

(noun) _____

(noun) _____

(plural noun) _____

(plural noun) _____

(noun) _____

(adjective) _____

(noun) _____

(noun) _____

(noun) _____

(adjective) _____

(verb) _____

(plural noun) _____

PICNIC

When going on a picnic, be sure to

_____ some _____ food.
　　(VERB)　　　　　　　　　　(ADJECTIVE)

You could pack some _____ and
　　　　　　　　　　　　　　　(NOUN)

_____ sandwiches, potato
　　(NOUN)

_____, baked _____,
　(PLURAL NOUN)　　　　　　　(PLURAL NOUN)

_____ cookies, and _____
　　(NOUN)　　　　　　　　　　　　(ADJECTIVE)

tea.

Pack all of the food inside a

_____, and take along a
(NOUN)

_____ to sit on. You may even
(NOUN)

want to take a _____ to play
(NOUN)

with.

Find a _____ place for your
(ADJECTIVE)

picnic. _____ your meal, being
(VERB)

careful that no _____ crawl into
(PLURAL NOUN)

your food and ruin your picnic!

WORD LIST

(plural noun) _____

(noun) _____

(adjective) _____

(noun) _____

(noun) _____

(adjective) _____

(adjective) _____

(noun) _____

(adjective) _____

(verb) _____

(plural noun) _____

(noun) _____

(noun) _____

(noun) _____

CLASSIC SONGS

_____ Keep Falling on My
(PLURAL NOUN)

_____
(NOUN)

_____ McDonald Had a _____
(ADJECTIVE)   (NOUN)

London _____ is Falling Down
(NOUN)

This _____ Man
(ADJECTIVE)

Mary Had a _____
(ADJECTIVE)

_____
(NOUN)

If You're _____ and You Know
(ADJECTIVE)

It, _____ Your _____
(VERB)   (PLURAL NOUN)

Row, Row, Row Your _____
(NOUN)

Pop Goes the _____
(NOUN)

Ring around the _____
(NOUN)

WORD LIST

(adjective) _____

(adjective)_____

(plural noun) _____

(number) _____

(adjective) _____

(adjective) _____

(adjective)_____

(noun)_____

(noun)_____

(noun)_____

(number)_____

(plural noun)_____

(number)_____

CLASSIC STORIES

_____ _____ Riding
    (ADJECTIVE)   (ADJECTIVE)
Hood

The Three Little _____
                      (PLURAL NOUN)

Goldilocks and the _____ Bears
                  (NUMBER)

_____ Beauty
    (ADJECTIVE)

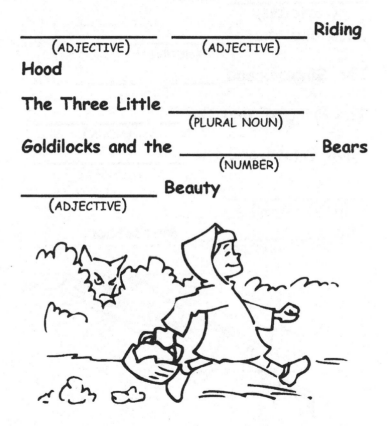

The _____ Mouse and the
(ADJECTIVE)

_____ Mouse
(ADJECTIVE)

Jack and the _____
(NOUN)

The Gingerbread _____
(NOUN)

The Princess and the _____
(NOUN)

Snow White and the _____
(NUMBER)

_____
(PLURAL NOUN)

The _____ Musketeers
(NUMBER)

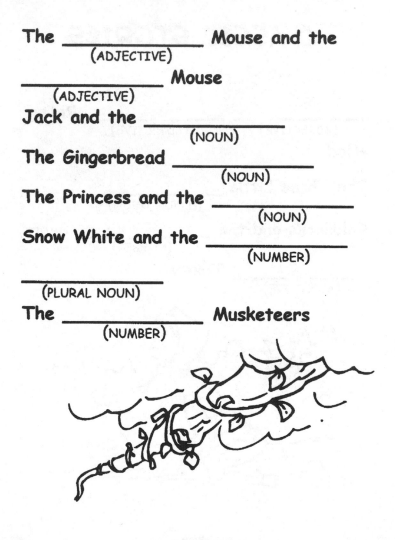

306

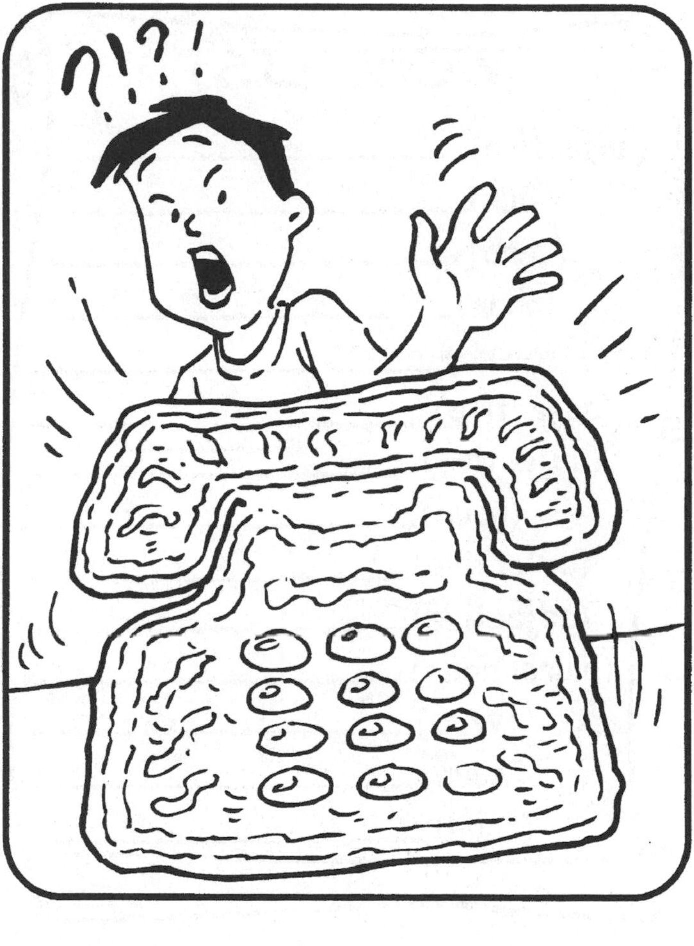

WORD LIST

(adjective) _____

(noun) _____

(verb) _____

(noun) _____

(verb) _____

(adjective) _____

(adjective) _____

(noun) _____

(adjective) _____

(adjective) _____

(plural noun) _____

(verb) _____

(noun) _____

(noun) _____

HELPING WITH MY BABY BROTHER

I help take care of my baby brother.

When he's _____, I put milk in
                    (ADJECTIVE)

a _____ for him. After he's
        (NOUN)

done, I _____ him by patting
            (VERB)

him on his _____.
                (NOUN)

Sometimes Mom asks me to _____
                                (VERB)

his _____ diaper. That can be
        (ADJECTIVE)

a _____ job!
    (ADJECTIVE)

At night, I help give him a _____.
                                (NOUN)

We make sure the water isn't too

_____ or too _____.
    (ADJECTIVE)   (ADJECTIVE)

After his bath, we put his _____
(PLURAL NOUN)
on him.

Before he goes to bed, I _____
(VERB)
with him, or read him a _____.
(NOUN)
Mom puts him in the _____ and
(NOUN)
we say good night.

WORD LIST

(noun) _____

(noun) _____

(noun) _____

(noun) _____

(adjective) _____

(noun) _____

LITTLE JACK HORNER

Little Jack Horner

Sat in a _____,
          (NOUN)

Eating a _____ pie;
          (NOUN)

He put in his _____,
               (NOUN)

And pulled out a _____,
                  (NOUN)

And said, "What a _____
                   (ADJECTIVE)

_____ am I!"
     (NOUN)

WORD LIST

(adjective) _____

(adjective) _____

(adjective) _____

(adjective) _____

(noun) _____

(noun) _____

(plural noun) _____

(number) _____

OLD KING COLE

Old King Cole

Was a _____ _____ soul,
        (ADJECTIVE)   (ADJECTIVE)

And a _____ _____
        (ADJECTIVE)   (ADJECTIVE)

soul was he;

He called for his _____,
                        (NOUN)

And he called for his _____,
                            (NOUN)

And he called for his _____
                            (PLURAL NOUN)

_____.
    (NUMBER)

WORD LIST

(verb "-ed") _____

(noun) _____

(adjective) _____

(noun) _____

(plural noun) _____

(plural noun) _____

HUMPTY DUMPTY

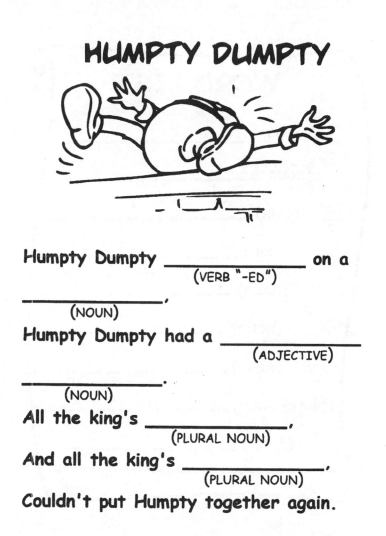

Humpty Dumpty _____ on a
(VERB "-ED")

_____,
(NOUN)

Humpty Dumpty had a _____
(ADJECTIVE)

_____.
(NOUN)

All the king's _____,
(PLURAL NOUN)

And all the king's _____,
(PLURAL NOUN)

Couldn't put Humpty together again.

WORD LIST

(verb) _____

(noun) _____

(noun) _____

(noun) _____

(noun) _____

(noun) _____

(noun) _____

(plural noun) _____

(noun) _____

LITTLE BOY BLUE

Little Boy Blue,

Come _____ your _____,
            (VERB)   (NOUN)

The _____'s in the
          (NOUN)

_____,
     (NOUN)

The _____'s in the
          (NOUN)

_____.
     (NOUN)

But where is the _____
                        (NOUN)

Who looks after the _____?
                          (PLURAL NOUN)

He's under a _____,
                   (NOUN)

Fast asleep.

WORD LIST

(noun) _____

(verb) _____

(adjective) _____

(noun) _____

(noun) _____

(adjective) _____

(adjective) _____

OLD MOTHER HUBBARD

Old Mother Hubbard

Went to the _____,
            (NOUN)

To _____ her _____ dog
   (VERB)   (ADJECTIVE)

a _____.
   (NOUN)

When she got there,

The _____ was _____,
      (NOUN)   (ADJECTIVE)

And so the _____ dog had none.
             (ADJECTIVE)

WORD LIST

(adjective) _____

(noun) _____

(adjective) _____

(adjective) _____

(verb) _____

(name of person) _____

(verb) _____

(adjective) _____

(name of person) _____

(adjective) _____

(number) _____

322

CLASSIC GAMES

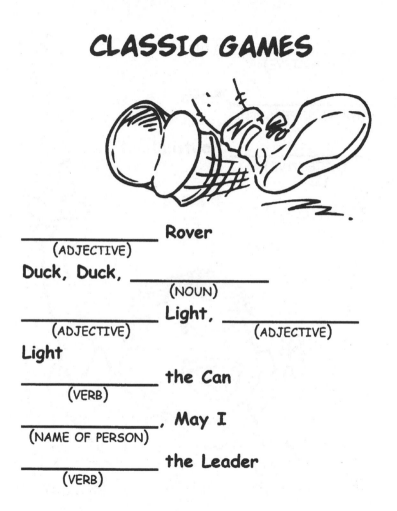

_____ **Rover**
(ADJECTIVE)

Duck, Duck, _____
(NOUN)

_____ **Light,** _____
(ADJECTIVE)   (ADJECTIVE)

Light

_____ **the Can**
(VERB)

_____, **May I**
(NAME OF PERSON)

_____ **the Leader**
(VERB)

_____ **Tag**
(ADJECTIVE)

_____ **Says**
(NAME OF PERSON)

_____ **Football**
(ADJECTIVE)

_____ **Square**
(NUMBER)

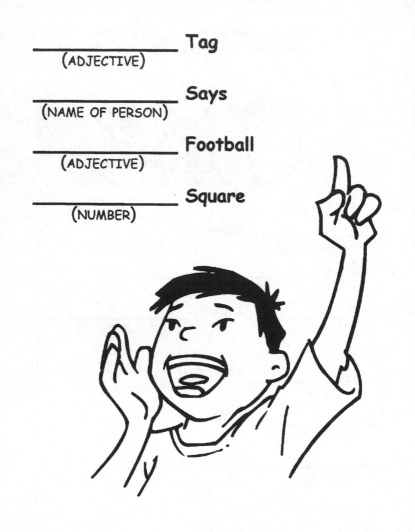

WORD LIST

(adjective) _____

(noun) _____

(plural noun) _____

(adjective) _____

(plural noun) _____

(adjective) _____

(plural noun) _____

(plural noun) _____

(plural noun) _____

(plural noun) _____

(adjective) _____

(plural noun) _____

(verb) _____

(adjective) _____

(adjective) _____

CHRISTMAS

Christmas is a _____ holiday,
(ADJECTIVE)
and there is lots to do to get ready!
Many people get a Christmas

_____, and decorate it with
(NOUN)

_____ and _____
(PLURAL NOUN)   (ADJECTIVE)
_____. This can be something
(PLURAL NOUN)

_____ that the family does
(ADJECTIVE)
together.

Some families bake _____
(PLURAL NOUN)
together. These can be cut out in shapes

of _____ or _____.
(PLURAL NOUN)   (PLURAL NOUN)

It's nice to share them with

_____.
(PLURAL NOUN)

On Christmas morning, children wake up

very _____. It's a good tradition
(ADJECTIVE)

to read the Christmas story before

opening _____. Be sure to
(PLURAL NOUN)

_____ those who give them to
(VERB)

you! Christmas is a _____ day,
(ADJECTIVE)

and many children go to bed feeling quite

_____. Through all of the fun,
(ADJECTIVE)

be sure to remember the true meaning of

the day!

WORD LIST

(adjective) _____

(adjective) _____

(plural noun) _____

(adjective) _____

(adjective) _____

(verb) _____

(verb) _____

(noun) _____

(noun) _____

(verb) _____

(noun) _____

(noun) _____

(adjective) _____

(adjective) _____

(plural noun) _____

(adjective) _____

SUMMER FUN

Summer months are _____!
                        (ADJECTIVE)
There's no school, and it's _____
                                  (ADJECTIVE)
enough outside to wear _____.
                            (PLURAL NOUN)
On _____ days, it's fun to go
      (ADJECTIVE)
to the _____ pool. I love to
          (ADJECTIVE)
_____ and _____ off
     (VERB)   (VERB)
the diving _____.
              (NOUN)

I also like to go to the _____ and
(NOUN)

_____ on the playground, ride
(VERB)

my _____, or throw a
(NOUN)

_____ with my friends.
(NOUN)

When it gets _____ outside, I
(ADJECTIVE)

catch _____ bugs and listen to
(ADJECTIVE)

the _____ chirping.
(PLURAL NOUN)

The summer months are my _____
(ADJECTIVE)

ones!

WORD LIST

(plural noun) _____

(plural noun) _____

(plural noun) _____

(liquid) _____

(verb) _____

(verb) _____

(plural noun) _____

(adjective) _____

(plural noun) _____

(noun) _____

(adjective) _____

(plural noun) _____

(adjective) _____

(adjective) _____

GETTING READY FOR BED

"Time for bed!" Dad says. "Please put

away your _____ and
(PLURAL NOUN)

_____, and I'll get you a snack
(PLURAL NOUN)

of _____ and _____."
(PLURAL NOUN)   (LIQUID)

When I'm finished, I _____
(VERB)

upstairs. I go into the bathroom to

_____ my face and brush my
(VERB)

_____. When I am
(PLURAL NOUN)

_____, I go to my room and
(ADJECTIVE)

put on my _____.
(PLURAL NOUN)

Finally, I crawl into my _____,
(NOUN)

feeling quite _____. After I
(ADJECTIVE)

pray, I pull up the _____,
(PLURAL NOUN)

ready for a _____ night's
(ADJECTIVE)

sleep, and _____ dreams.
(ADJECTIVE)

WORD LIST

(noun) _____

(number) _____

(plural noun) _____

(number) _____

(noun) _____

(number) _____

(noun) _____

(number) _____

(adjective) _____

(noun) _____

(noun) _____

BAA, BAA, BLACK SHEEP

Baa, baa, black sheep,

Have you any _____?
                  (NOUN)

Yes, sir, yes, sir,

_____ _____ full.
   (NUMBER)   (PLURAL NOUN)

_____ for the _____,
   (NUMBER)   (NOUN)

And _____ for the _____,
        (NUMBER)   (NOUN)

And _____ for the _____
        (NUMBER)   (ADJECTIVE)

_____
   (NOUN)

Who lives down the _____.
                          (NOUN)

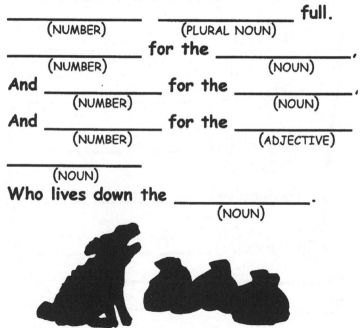

WORD LIST

(adjective)_____

(noun)_____

(verb)_____

(adjective) _____

(adjective)_____

(adjective)_____

(plural noun) _____

MARY, MARY, QUITE CONTRARY

Mary, Mary, quite _____,
(ADJECTIVE)

How does your _____
(NOUN)

_____?
(VERB)

With _____ bells and
(ADJECTIVE)

_____ shells
(ADJECTIVE)

And _____ _____ all
(ADJECTIVE)   (PLURAL NOUN)

in a row.

WORD LIST

(noun) _____

(noun) _____

(noun) _____

(verb) _____

(noun) _____

(noun) _____

(verb) _____

(noun) _____

(noun) _____

ROCK-A-BYE, BABY

Rock-a-bye, baby, on the _____
(NOUN)
top;

When the _____ blows, the
(NOUN)
_____ will _____;
(NOUN)   (VERB)
When the _____ breaks, the
(NOUN)
_____ will _____;
(NOUN)   (VERB)
Down will come _____,
(NOUN)
_____ and all.
(NOUN)

WORD LIST

(adjective) _____

(plural noun) _____

(verb) _____

(verb) _____

(verb) _____

(verb "-ing") _____

(plural noun) _____

LITTLE BO-PEEP

_____ Bo-Peep has lost her
(ADJECTIVE)

_____,
(PLURAL NOUN)

And doesn't know where to _____
(VERB)

them.

_____ them along, and they'll
(VERB)

_____ home
(VERB)

_____ their _____
(VERB "-ING")   (PLURAL NOUN)

behind them.

WORD LIST

(plural noun) _____

(plural noun) _____

(number) _____

(liquid) _____

(number) _____

(noun) _____

(noun) _____

(verb "-ing") _____

(verb "-ing") _____

(verb "-ing") _____

(plural noun) _____

(number) _____

HOW TO STAY HEALTHY

To stay healthy, you should:

1. Eat plenty of _____ and
   (PLURAL NOUN)

   _____.
   (PLURAL NOUN)

2. Drink at least _____ glasses of
   (NUMBER)

   _____ each day.
   (LIQUID)

3. Brush your teeth _____ times each day.
   (NUMBER)

4. Turn on the _____ while reading.
   (NOUN)

5. Limit the amount of time watching

   _____.
   (NOUN)

6. Get exercise. This can include _____,
   (VERB "-ING")

   _____, _____.
   (VERB "-ING")   (VERB "-ING")

7. Wash your _____ often.
   (PLURAL NOUN)

8. Get at least _____ hours of sleep
   (NUMBER)

   each night.

WORD LIST

(adjective) _____

(verb) _____

(adjective) _____

(verb) _____

(number) _____

(verb) _____

(plural noun) _____

(adjective) _____

(verb) _____

(adjective) _____

(exclamation) _____

(adjective) _____

(adjective) _____

(noun) _____

(noun) _____

348

RAINY DAYS

On rainy days, I like to find something

_____ to do. Although I'd rather
(ADJECTIVE)

_____ outside, there are some
(VERB)

fun things to do inside.

I like to choose a _____ book to
(ADJECTIVE)

_____. I have at least
(VERB)

_____ to choose from!
(NUMBER)

Sometimes I _____ on the
(VERB)

computer. I can play _____, or
(PLURAL NOUN)

I can look up some _____ facts
(ADJECTIVE)

and information.

I also like to _____ pictures.
(VERB)

Mom and Dad say that I'm a

_____ artist, and when they see
(ADJECTIVE)

my finished picture, they say,

"_____! You are quite talented!"
(EXCLAMATION)

It's always fun when Mom or Dad makes

me something _____ to eat. My
(ADJECTIVE)

favorite rainy day meal is _____
(ADJECTIVE)

_____ sandwiches and
(NOUN)

_____ soup.
(NOUN)

WORD LIST

(name of song) _____

(adjective) _____

(number) _____

(name of person) _____

(verb) _____

(name of person) _____

(name of song) _____

(noun) _____

(adjective) _____

(adjective) _____

(number) _____

(adjective) _____

THE TALENT SHOW

Each year, our school has a talent show.
This year, I will be singing _____.
(NAME OF SONG)
It is a _____ song, and I have
(ADJECTIVE)
been practicing it for _____ weeks!
(NUMBER)
My friend _____ will _____
(NAME OF PERSON)   (VERB)
a poem, and _____ will be playing
(NAME OF PERSON)
_____ on the _____. During
(NAME OF SONG)   (NOUN)
practice, it sounded _____!
(ADJECTIVE)
We all feel a little bit _____,
(ADJECTIVE)
because there will be at least _____
(NUMBER)
people there. But we will do our best, and
it will be a _____ talent show.
(ADJECTIVE)

WORD LIST

(name of person) _____

(number) _____

(number) _____

(adjective) _____

(noun) _____

(noun) _____

(verb) _____

(number) _____

(noun) _____

(noun) _____

(adjective) _____

(adjective) _____

BASEBALL

My favorite sport is baseball. I think

_____ is the best player!
(NAME OF PERSON)

I am on a team with _____ other
(NUMBER)

players. We play _____ games
(NUMBER)

each week. We always have

a _____ time together.
(ADJECTIVE)

At our last game, I took my

_____ and stepped up to home
(NOUN)

_____. I was ready to
(NOUN)

_____ the ball out of the park!
(VERB)

I was disappointed when I heard the

umpire call, "Strike _____!"
(NUMBER)

But my _____ told me that I
(NOUN)

did my best, and that's what is

important.

After the game, we all went out to eat

_____. We had a _____
(NOUN)   (ADJECTIVE)

time, and I went home feeling quite

_____.
(ADJECTIVE)

PG. 9

PG. 11

" LOVE IS PATIENT , LOVE IS KIND . IT DOES NOT ENVY , IT DOES NOT BOAST, IT IS NOT PROUD . IT IS NOT RUDE , IT IS NOT SELF - SEEKING , IT IS NOT EASILY ANGERED , IT KEEPS NO RECORD OF WRONGS . LOVE DOES NOT DELIGHT IN EVIL BUT REJOICES WITH THE TRUTH . IT ALWAYS PROTECTS , ALWAYS TRUSTS , ALWAYS HOPES , ALWAYS PERSEVERES . "

1 CORINTHIANS 13:4—7

1. (S) P I R I T
2. D E L (I) G H T
3. E (N) T I R E
4. U (N) I T Y
5. P E R F (E) C T
6. (R) E C O R D
7. (S) E E K

"BUT GOD DEMONSTRATES HIS OWN LOVE FOR US IN THIS: WHILE WE WERE STILL S I N N E R S , CHRIST DIED FOR US."

ROMANS 5:8

1. T R U T (H)
2. F O R G (A) V E
3. F A T H E (R)
4. T I M (I) D I T Y

"LOVE DOES NO H A R M TO ITS NEIGHBOR. THEREFORE LOVE IS THE FULFILLMENT OF THE LAW."

ROMANS 13:10

" YOU , MY BROTHERS , WERE CALLED TO BE FREE . BUT DO NOT USE YOUR FREEDOM TO INDULGE THE SINFUL NATURE ; RATHER , SERVE ONE ANOTHER IN LOVE . THE ENTIRE LAW IS SUMMED UP IN A SINGLE COMMAND : ' LOVE YOUR NEIGHBOR AS YOURSELF .'"

GALATIANS 5:13–14

" BEAR WITH EACH OTHER AND FORGIVE WHATEVER GRIEVANCES YOU MAY HAVE AGAINST ONE ANOTHER . FORGIVE AS THE LORD FORGAVE YOU . AND OVER ALL THESE VIRTUES PUT ON LOVE , WHICH BINDS THEM ALL TOGETHER IN PERFECT UNITY ."

COLOSSIANS 3:13–14

1. (S) I N F U L
2. (P) R I D E
3. V (I) R T U E
4. A N G E (R)
5. S (I) N
6. (T) R E E

"FOR GOD DID NOT GIVE US A SPIRIT OF TIMIDITY, BUT A S P I R I T OF POWER, OF LOVE AND OF SELF-DISCIPLINE."

2TIMOTHY 1:7

" HOW   GREAT   IS   THE
LOVE   THE   FATHER
HAS   LAVISHED   ON
US ,   THAT   WE   SHOULD
BE   CALLED   CHILDREN
OF   GOD | AND   THAT
IS   WHAT   WE   ARE |
THE   REASON   THE
WORLD   DOES   NOT
KNOW   US   IS   THAT
IT   DID   NOT   KNOW
HIM ."

1 JOHN 3:1

" THIS   IS   HOW   WE   KNOW
WHAT   LOVE   IS :   JESUS
CHRIST   LAID   DOWN
HIS   LIFE   FOR   US .
AND   WE   OUGHT   TO
LAY   DOWN   OUR   LIVES
FOR   OUR   BROTHERS ."

1 JOHN 3:16

1. (W) H O
2. R E J (O) I C E
3. D E A (R)
4. (D) E L I G H T
5. (S) O U L

"DEAR CHILDREN, LET US NOT LOVE
WITH W O R D S OR TONGUE BUT
WITH ACTIONS AND IN TRUTH."

1JOHN 3:18

"   DEAR   FRIENDS ,   LET
US   LOVE   ONE   ANOTHER ,
FOR   LOVE   COMES   FROM   GOD .
EVERYONE   WHO   LOVES
HAS   BEEN   BORN   OF
GOD   AND   KNOWS   GOD .
WHOEVER   DOES   NOT
LOVE   DOES   NOT   KNOW
GOD ,   BECAUSE   GOD   IS
LOVE ."

1 JOHN 4:7-8

" THERE IS NO FEAR
IN LOVE . BUT PERFECT
LOVE DRIVES OUT
FEAR , BECAUSE FEAR
HAS TO DO WITH
PUNISHMENT . THE
ONE WHO FEARS IS
NOT MADE PERFECT
IN LOVE ."

1 JOHN 4:18

THINK
THINK
THINK

1. W O R L D
2. T O N G U E
3. J E S U S
4. O U G H T
5. H I S
6. C O M P L E T E
7. H O P E

"THEN MY SOUL WILL R E J O I C E
IN THE LORD AND DELIGHT IN HIS
SALVATION."

PSALM 35:9

" THEN WILL I GO TO THE ALTAR OF GOD, TO GOD, MY JOY AND MY DELIGHT . I WILL PRAISE YOU WITH THE HARP , O GOD , MY GOD ."

PSALM 43:4

1. (C) H R I S T
2. L (O) V E
3. F R O (M)
4. (P) O W E R
5. D E A (L)
6. F (E) A R
7. A (C) T I O N
8. H (E) A R T

"I HAVE TOLD YOU THIS SO THAT MY JOY MAY BE IN YOU AND THAT YOUR JOY MAY BE C O M P L E T E ."

JOHN 15:11

" MAY THE GOD OF HOPE FILL YOU WITH ALL JOY AND PEACE AS YOU TRUST IN HIM , SO THAT YOU MAY OVERFLOW WITH HOPE BY THE POWER OF THE HOLY SPIRIT ."

ROMANS 15:13

" IF YOU HAVE ANY ENCOURAGEMENT FROM BEING UNITED WITH CHRIST , IF ANY COMFORT FROM HIS LOVE , IF ANY FELLOWSHIP WITH THE SPIRIT , IF ANY TENDERNESS AND COMPASSION , THEN MAKE MY JOY COMPLETE BY BEING LIKE - MINDED , HAVING THE SAME LOVE , BEING ONE IN SPIRIT AND PURPOSE ."

PHILIPPIANS 2:1-2

"YOU BECAME IMITATORS OF US AND OF THE LORD : IN SPITE OF SEVERE SUFFERING , YOU WELCOMED THE MESSAGE WITH THE JOY . GIVEN BY THE HOLY SPIRIT ."

1 THESSALONIANS 1:6

1. I S R A E L
2. S H A M E
3. U N I T E D
4. S C O R N
5. T H R O N E
6. R E F R E S H

"YOUR LOVE HAS GIVEN ME GREAT JOY AND ENCOURAGEMENT, BECAUSE YOU, BROTHER, HAVE REFRESHED THE HEARTS OF THE S A I N T S."

PHILEMON 1:7

" LET US FIX OUR EYES ON JESUS , THE AUTHOR AND PERFECTER OF OUR FAITH , WHO FOR THE JOY SET BEFORE HIM ENDURED THE CROSS , SCORNING ITS SHAME , AND SAT DOWN AT THE RIGHT HAND OF THE THRONE OF GOD ."

HEBREWS 12:2

1. A U (T) H O R
2. W O (R) L D
3. J (O) Y
4. T R O (U) B L E
5. (B) E I N G
6. W E (L) C O M E
7. S P I T (E)
8. (D) O W N

"PEACE I LEAVE WITH YOU; MY PEACE I GIVE YOU. I DO NOT GIVE TO YOU AS THE WORLD GIVES. DO NOT LET YOUR HEARTS BE T R O U B L E D AND DO NOT BE AFRAID."

JOHN 14:27

"'I HAVE TOLD YOU THESE THINGS , SO THAT IN ME YOU MAY HAVE PEACE . IN THIS WORLD YOU WILL HAVE TROUBLE . BUT TAKE HEART ! I HAVE OVERCOME THE WORLD .'"

JOHN 16:33

1. H I (M)
2. (E) N C O U R A G E
3. N E W (S)
4. J E (S) U S
5. F (A) I T H
6. (G) I V E
7. S A M (E)

"YOU KNOW THE M E S S A G E GOD SENT TO THE PEOPLE OF ISRAEL, TELLING THE GOOD NEWS OF PEACE THROUGH JESUS CHRIST, WHO IS LORD OF ALL."

ACTS 10:36

1. O V E R (C) O M E
2. (H) E A R T
3. L O (R) D
4. F E L L O W S H (I) P
5. (S) O N
6. R I G H (T)

"GRACE AND PEACE TO YOU FROM GOD OUR FATHER AND FROM THE LORD JESUS C H R I S T ."

ROMANS 1:7

1. (P) O W E R
2. O V E (E) F L O W
3. (C) A L L E D
4. (C) H R I S T I A N
5. E V (E) R

"THEREFORE, SINCE WE HAVE BEEN JUSTIFIED THROUGH FAITH, WE HAVE P E A C E WITH GOD THROUGH OUR LORD JESUS CHRIST."

ROMANS 5:1

1. H E A R T (S)
2. M (I) N D
3. (N) O B L E
4. F U L (F) I L L
5. (U) N D O
6. R O V E (L) Y

"THE MIND OF S I N F U L MAN IS DEATH, BUT THE MIND CONTROLLED BY THE SPIRIT IS LIFE AND PEACE."

ROMANS 8:6

1. (D) E N Y
2. M E M B (E) R S
3. (P) L A C E
4. H O P (E)
5. M I (N) D
6. G U A R (D)
7. (S) A V E D

"IF IT IS POSSIBLE, AS FAR AS IT D E P E N D S ON YOU, LIVE AT PEACE WITH EVERYONE."

ROMANS 12:18

1. (E) D I F Y
2. C A R E (F) U L
3. (F) O L L O W
4. B (O) N D
5. (R) I G H T E O U S
6. I N H E R I (T)

"LET US THEREFORE MAKE EVERY E F F O R T TO DO WHAT LEADS TO PEACE AND TO MUTUAL EDIFICATION."

ROMANS 14:19

" MAY THE GOD OF HOPE FILL YOU WITH ALL JOY AND PEACE AS YOU TRUST IN HIM , SO THAT YOU MAY OVERFLOW WITH HOPE BY THE POWER OF THE HOLY SPIRIT ."

ROMANS 15:13

1. (H) O L Y
2. J (O) Y
3. R U (L) E
4. J U S T (I) F Y
5. G E (N) T L E
6. F A T H (E) R
7. W I (S) D O M
8. (S) H O W N

"MAKE EVERY EFFORT TO LIVE IN PEACE WITH ALL MEN AND TO BE HOLY; WITHOUT H O L I N E S S NO ONE WILL SEE THE LORD."

HEBREWS 12:14

1. J O Y F (U) L
2. M I (N) D
3. K (I) N G D O M
4. P R O P H E (T)
5. (Y) O U R S E L F

"MAKE EVERY EFFORT TO KEEP THE U N I T Y OF THE SPIRIT THROUGH THE BOND OF PEACE."

EPHESIANS 4:3

1. E F F O R (T)
2. L O (R) D
3. S (A) I N T S
4. K I (N) D
5. (S) P E A K
6. O V E R (C) O M E
7. H (E) A V E N
8. (N) A M E
9. B O (D) Y
10. C H O (S) E N

"AND THE PEACE OF GOD, WHICH
T R A N S C E N D S ALL
UNDERSTANDING, WILL GUARD YOUR
HEARTS AND YOUR MINDS IN CHRIST
JESUS."

PHILIPPIANS 4:7

" LET   THE   PEACE   OF

CHRIST   RULE   IN

YOUR   HEARTS ,   SINCE

AS   MEMBERS   OF   ONE

BODY   YOU   WERE

CALLED   TO   PEACE

AND   BE   THANKFUL ."

COLOSSIANS 3:15

1. (H) E A R T
2. P A T I (E) N C E
3. P R O (M) I S E
4. T H A N K (S)
5. W R O T (E)
6. S A (L) V A T I O N
7. (F) I L L

"NOW MAY THE LORD OF PEACE
H I M S E L F GIVE YOU PEACE
AT ALL TIMES AND IN EVERY WAY. THE
LORD BE WITH ALL OF YOU."

2THESSALONIANS 3:16

" THEREFORE , AS GOD'S CHOSEN PEOPLE , HOLY AND DEARLY LOVED , CLOTHE YOURSELVES WITH COMPASSION , KINDNESS , HUMILITY , GENTLENESS AND PATIENCE ."

COLOSSIANS 3:12

" BUT FOR THAT VERY REASON I WAS SHOWN MERCY SO THAT IN ME , THE WORST OF SINNERS , CHRIST JESUS MIGHT DISPLAY HIS UNLIMITED PATIENCE AS AN EXAMPLE FOR THOSE WHO WOULD BELIEVE ON HIM AND RECEIVE ETERNAL LIFE ."

1 TIMOTHY 1:16

" PREACH THE WORD ; BE PREPARED IN SEASON AND OUT OF SEASON ; CORRECT , REBUKE AND ENCOURAGE — WITH GREAT PATIENCE AND CAREFUL INSTRUCTION ."

2 TIMOTHY 4:2

1. H U M **I** L I T Y
2. C O N **V** I N C E
3. S T R E N G T **H**
4. R **E** P E N T
5. S T E **R** N
6. C H **I** L D
7. L I G H **T**

"WE DO NOT WANT YOU TO BECOME LAZY, BUT TO IMITATE THOSE WHO THROUGH FAITH AND PATIENCE I N H E R I T WHAT HAS BEEN PROMISED."

HEBREWS 6:12

1. P L E A **S** E S
2. **P** R O V I D E D
3. **G** O D L Y
4. **K** N O W L E D G E
5. D I V I N **E**

"BROTHERS, AS AN EXAMPLE OF PATIENCE IN THE FACE OF SUFFERING, TAKE THE PROPHETS WHO S P O K E IN THE NAME OF THE LORD."

JAMES 5:10

" BEAR IN MIND THAT OUR LORD'S PATIENCE MEANS SALVATION , JUST AS OUR DEAR BROTHER PAUL ALSO WROTE YOU WITH THE WISDOM THAT GOD GAVE HIM "

2 PETER 3:15

1. (K)N O W I N G
2. P A T (I) E N C E
3. B O R (N)
4. (D) O W N
5. C H I L D R E (N)
6. P E A C (E)
7. P R A I (S) E
8. (S) P I R I T

"'I HAVE LOVED YOU WITH AN EVER-LASTING LOVE; I HAVE DRAWN YOU WITH LOVING- K I N D N E S S .'"

JEREMIAH 31:3

" YET HE HAS NOT LEFT HIMSELF WITHOUT TESTIMONY : HE HAS SHOWN KINDNESS BY GIVING YOU RAIN FROM HEAVEN AND CROPS IN THEIR SEASONS ; HE PROVIDES YOU WITH PLENTY OF FOOD AND FILLS YOUR HEARTS WITH JOY ."

ACTS 14:17

1. L O (R) D
2. F (A) I T H
3. K (I) N D N E S S
4. R E (N) E W A L
5. B (I) R T H
6. (N) E E D
7. (G) O O D

"THE ISLANDERS SHOWED US UNUSUAL KINDNESS. THEY BUILT A FIRE AND WELCOMED US ALL BECAUSE IT WAS R A I N I N G AND COLD."

ACTS 28:2

" OR DO YOU SHOW CONTEMPT FOR THE RICHES OF HIS KINDNESS , TOLERANCE AND PATIENCE , NOT REALIZING THAT GOD'S KINDNESS LEADS YOU TOWARD REPENTANCE ?"

ROMANS 2:4

" CONSIDER THEREFORE THE KINDNESS AND STERNNESS OF GOD : STERNNESS TO THOSE WHO FELL , BUT KINDNESS TO YOU , PROVIDED THAT YOU CONTINUE IN HIS KINDNESS . OTHERWISE , YOU ALSO WILL BE CUT OFF ."

ROMANS 11:22

" BUT WHEN THE KINDNESS AND LOVE OF GOD OUR SAVIOR APPEARED , HE SAVED US , NOT BECAUSE OF RIGHTEOUS THINGS WE HAD DONE , BUT BECAUSE OF HIS MERCY . HE SAVED US THROUGH THE WASHING OF REBIRTH AND RENEWAL BY THE HOLY SPIRIT ."

TITUS 3:4–5

1. C O L D
2. L I G H T
3. L O V E
4. C O N S I S T
5. R E A S O N
6. G O D

"I AM STILL CONFIDENT OF THIS: I WILL SEE THE GOODNESS OF THE LORD IN THE LAND OF THE L I V I N G ."

PSALM 27:13

" I MYSELF AM CONVINCED , MY BROTHERS , THAT YOU YOURSELVES ARE FULL OF GOODNESS , COMPLETE IN KNOWLEDGE AND COMPETENT TO INSTRUCT ONE ANOTHER ."

ROMANS 15:14

" FOR YOU WERE ONCE DARKNESS , BUT NOW YOU ARE LIGHT IN THE LORD . LIVE AS CHILDREN OF LIGHT (FOR THE FRUIT OF THE LIGHT CONSISTS IN ALL GOODNESS , RIGHTEOUSNESS AND TRUTH) AND FIND OUT WHAT PLEASES THE LORD ."

EPHESIANS 5:8–10

" FOR THIS VERY REASON , MAKE EVERY EFFORT TO ADD TO YOUR FAITH GOODNESS ; AND TO GOODNESS , KNOWLEDGE : AND TO KNOWLEDGE SELF - CONTROL ; AND TO SELF - CONTROL , PERSEVERANCE ; AND TO PERSEVERANCE GODLINESS : AND TO GODLINESS , BROTHERLY KINDNESS : AND TO BROTHERLY KINDNESS , LOVE ."

2 PETER 1:5-7

THINK THINK THINK

" IT IS GOOD TO PRAISE THE LORD AND MAKE MUSIC TO YOUR NAME , O MOST HIGH , TO PROCLAIM YOUR LOVE IN THE MORNING AND YOUR FAITHFULNESS AT NIGHT , TO THE MUSIC OF THE TEN - STRINGED LYRE AND THE MELODY OF THE HARP ."

PSALM 92:1-3

1. (F) L E E
2. B R (O) T H E R
3. G (R) E A T
4. C L O T H (E)
5. L O (V) E D
6. (E) N D U R E S
7. C H (R) I S T

"FOR THE LORD IS GOOD AND HIS LOVE ENDURES F O R E V E R : HIS FAITHFULNESS CONTINUES THROUGH ALL GENERATIONS."

PSALM 100:5

1. T R U (T) H
2. D E (A) R L Y
3. (B) I N D
4. A P P E A (L)
5. P (E) O P L E
6. H U M I L I (T) Y

"LET LOVE AND FAITHFULNESS NEVER LEAVE YOU; BIND THEM AROUND YOUR NECK, WRITE THEM ON THE T A B L E T OF YOUR HEART."

PROVERBS 3:3

"' FOR I , THE LORD , LOVE JUSTICE ; I HATE ROBBERY AND INIQUITY . IN MY FAITHFULNESS I WILL REWARD THEM AND MAKE AN EVERLASTING COVENANT WITH THEM .'"

ISAIAH 61:8

" WHAT IF SOME DID NOT HAVE FAITH ? WILL THEIR LACK OF FAITH NULLIFY GOD'S FAITHFULNESS ? NOT AT ALL | LET GOD BE TRUE , AND EVERY MAN A LIAR ."

ROMANS 3:3—4

" IT GAVE ME GREAT JOY TO HAVE SOME BROTHERS COME AND TELL ABOUT YOUR FAITHFULNESS TO THE TRUTH AND HOW YOU CONTINUE TO WALK IN THE TRUTH ."

3 JOHN 1:3

THINK THINK THINK

" BY THE MEEKNESS AND GENTLENESS OF CHRIST , I APPEAL TO YOU — I, PAUL, WHO AM 'TIMID' WHEN FACE TO FACE WITH YOU, BUT 'BOLD' WHEN AWAY !"

2 CORINTHIANS 10:1

" THEREFORE , AS GOD'S CHOSEN PEOPLE , HOLY AND DEARLY LOVED , CLOTHE YOURSELVES WITH COMPASSION , KINDNESS , HUMILITY , GENTLENESS AND PATIENCE ."

COLOSSIANS 3:12

" BUT YOU , MAN OF GOD , FLEE FROM ALL THIS , AND PURSUE RIGHTEOUSNESS , GODLINESS , FAITH , LOVE , ENDURANCE AND GENTLENESS ."

1 TIMOTHY 6:11

" BUT IN YOUR HEARTS SET APART CHRIST AS LORD . ALWAYS BE PREPARED TO GIVE AN ANSWER TO EVERYONE WHO ASKS YOU TO GIVE THE REASON FOR THE HOPE THAT YOU HAVE . BUT DO THIS WITH GENTLENESS AND RESPECT ."

1 PETER 3:15

THINK THINK THINK

" __MAKE__ __IT__ __YOUR__ __AMBITION__ __TO__ __LEAD__ __A__ __QUIET__ __LIFE__, __TO__ __MIND__ __YOUR__ __OWN__ __BUSINESS__ __AND__ __TO__ __WORK__ __WITH__ __YOUR__ __HANDS__, __JUST__ __AS__ __WE__ __TOLD__ __YOU__, __SO__ __THAT__ __YOUR__ __DAILY__ __LIFE__ __MAY__ __WIN__ __THE__ __RESPECT__ __OF__ __OUTSIDERS__ __AND__ __SO__ __THAT__ __YOU__ __WILL__ __NOT__ __BE__ __DEPENDENT__ __ON__ __ANYBODY__ "

1 THESSALONIANS 4:11-12

1. E F F O R (T)
2. A M B (I) T I O N
3. (M) E N
4. Q U (I) E T
5. D E P E N (D)
6. L (I) F E
7. (T) O L D
8. B O D (Y)

"FOR GOD DID NOT GIVE US A SPIRIT OF __T I M I D I T Y__, BUT A SPIRIT OF POWER, OF LOVE AND OF SELF-DISCIPLINE."

2 TIMOTHY 1:7

1. (R) E J O I C E
2. F R E (E) D O M
3. (S) E L F
4. (P) R O U D
5. O N (E)
6. (C) R E A T E
7. N A (T) U R E

"TEACH THE OLDER MEN TO BE TEMPERATE, WORTHY OF __R E S P E C T__, SELF-CONTROLLED, AND SOUND IN FAITH, IN LOVE AND IN ENDURANCE. ."

TITUS 2:2

" IT IS NOT GOOD
TO EAT TOO MUCH
HONEY , NOR IS IT
HONORABLE TO SEEK
ONE'S OWN HONOR .
LIKE A CITY
WHOSE WALLS ARE
BROKEN DOWN IS
A MAN WHO LACKS
SELF - CONTROL ."

PROVERBS 25:27-28

THINK
THINK
THINK